LAUREL & HARDY

D1489066

series edited and designed by Ian Cameron

LAUREL & HARDY

CHARLES BARR

UNIVERSITY OF CALIFORNIA PRESS

Produced by Design Yearbook Limited for Movie Magazine Limited, 21 Ivor Place, London, N.W.1.

Published in the United States and Canada by the University of California Press, Berkeley 94720.

First American edition 1968.

Second Printing, 1974
ISBN:0-520-00085-4

Library of Congress Catalog Card No 68- 31074
Printed in the United States of America

Author's Acknowledgements
In writing on film-makers as prolific as Laurel and Hardy (nearly 100 of whose films are in circulation) one is especially dependent on the goodwill of others. Among distributors my first debt is to Watsofilms of Coventry, and specifically to Arthur Waring, for letting me borrow freely from their 16 mm stock. I have drawn on them for some 25 shorts and for the following features: Pardon Us, Pack up your Troubles, Sons of the Desert, Our Relations, Blockheads, Flying Deuces, A Chump at Oxford *and* Saps at Sea. I am also grateful to Ron Harris Ltd for lending Fra Diavolo, *to* Kingston Film Hire *for some shorts and for* Atoll K, *to* Grand National Films *for some material on* 35 mm, *and to* Philip Jenkinson. For projection facilities I am indebted to Corgarff Castle Films, and to Eric Sprawson and Douglas Livsey. I have been greatly helped by members of the British Film Institute staff in the Information, Library and Education departments; also by Colin Ford, and the staff at the National Film Archive. For further help I am grateful to Freddie Stockdale, Michael Dibb, Joyce Pirie, and Anne Morris. Finally I wish to thank Victor Perkins for his generous assistance at a number of points, not least for reading the text in proof and making some valuable suggestions.
Westow, November 1967

Cover: Pack up your Troubles.

Frontispiece: Hog Wild—*the car is crushed between two tramcars but still goes.*

Editor's Acknowledgements
Stills by courtesy of John Kobal, Metro-Goldwyn-Mayer, Twentieth Century-Fox, United Artists, National Film Archive, R.K.O. Radio, Screenspace.

Our thanks are due particularly to Screenspace and to Stanley Hart for their co-operation.

CONTENTS

NOTE: Picture sequences always read from left to right, even cross double-page spreads.

INTRODUCTION

Arthur C. Clarke has a short story called *Expedition To Earth* in which beings from Venus discover, on a long-dead Earth, a single can of film. Their scientists devise a machine to project it; historians and psychologists study the film and inaugurate a programme of research into this relic of a civilisation of which they have hitherto known nothing.

' For the rest of time it would symbolise the human race. . . . Thousands of books would be written about it. Millions of times in the ages to come those last few words would flash across the screen:

A Walt Disney Production'

End of story—and one should point out that this was before Disney moved away from cartoons, so it is Donald Duck on screen, not Hayley Mills.

To some, the irony might seem no less if it were a Laurel and Hardy film, yet I am not sure that, in the pleasant game of picking one film suitable to teach aliens about the human race, I would not choose a Laurel and Hardy short. They are the most universal of comics, in range as in appeal, and how can one understand Man without understanding his humour ? It is not only that such films as *Scram*, *The Music Box* and *Big Business* actually show laughter as well as arousing it, but that they give us in so clear a form so much of the human condition: pain and joy, authority and subversion, aspiration and disaster, generosity and ill-will, with the directness of allegory. Indeed, all these forces are located in Laurel and Hardy themselves. Hardy never for long ceases to be subservient to authority even when he undermines it, nor to be shocked by violence even when himself exercising it. They are

supreme liberators from bourgeois inhibitions, yet essentially they are, or aspire to be, respectable bourgeois citizens. For all the appealing predictability in their films, their feelings and attitudes are not yet hardened to a crust but preserve the fluidity, the 'overlapping' quality, the moment-to-moment inconsistencies of childhood. This is why they can play so many different roles, householders and vagrants, criminals and policemen, without undergoing change. Their 'Everyman' quality helps to explain the universality of their appeal. It is safe to say that no-one in films has been loved so universally and for so long as Laurel and Hardy. They still seem to be the first comedians to attract children, and the last of whom adults tire; for all the (perhaps merciful) contempt shown for them by many intellectuals, they have never lost their popularity, even while, after 1940, they were turning out inferior films. Their work is still revived successfully on television, and one need only start to project a Laurel and Hardy for an audience, whether of children, film technicians, schoolmasters, anyone, to accumulate as if from nowhere.

Their very 'elementality' makes it hard to write of them without being ponderous, trying to reduce to manageable formulae the irreducible. The critic finds himself in the position of the policeman in *Big Business*, who arrives, with notebook, in the middle of a war between James Finlayson on the one hand and Laurel and Hardy on the other. He is systematically destroying their car while they destroy his house. Through most of the picture, each side acts alternately while the other looks on with cool interest at the destruc-

tion, not trying to intervene. What can one report about such a scene, at once monstrously unrealistic and psychologically profound? There is a marvellous discrepancy between the actors' continued activity and the policeman's immobility (to which we return in cut-away shots), and between the inexorable progression of their work and the occasional convulsive notes he is moved to write—as if any one of their acts of destruction were more shocking than the rest. The notebook cannot order the scene, nor can he cope with them when finally he intervenes: as they mime their explanations to him, Laurel and Hardy burst into tears, and these tears infect in succession Finlayson, the policeman, and the spectators. With everyone now committed to a very moral lament for these anti-social happenings, Hardy nudges Laurel and they both laugh. The policeman sees them and gives chase. The cigar which Laurel has given Finlayson as a peace offering explodes in his face. Tears, laughter, anger are given their purest, irreducible form, and the film is as good as a documentary about them, apart from everything else that it is. What better film to preserve for the Venusians?

Frames: **Big Business** *with Tiny Sanford.*

EARLY CAREER

Stan Laurel was born Arthur Stanley Jefferson in 1890, in Lancashire. Oliver Hardy was born Norvell Hardy in 1892, in Georgia. Like the other supreme partnership of the 1920s, Hobbs and Sutcliffe, they came together casually, relatively late in their professional careers. The first official Laurel and Hardy film, *Putting Pants on Philip*, was shot in 1927. Their films divide roughly into five groups:
the films which they acted in together before this
silent films made as a team between 1927 and 1929
sound shorts between 1929 and 1935
feature films between 1931 and 1940
feature films after 1940 (made under entirely different conditions).

After 1945 they made only one film together; this was shot in France and had only a limited release. They continued to make some stage appearances, and Hardy did some minor film work on his own. Hardy died in 1957, and Laurel in 1965.

Laurel worked from an early age in English vaudeville. He went on tours to America in 1910 (in a company which included Chaplin) and in 1913, after which he stayed on permanently, though he was never to give up his British citizenship.

In 1917 he made his first film, *Nuts in May*, and soon after this appeared for the first time with Oliver Hardy in a film called *Lucky Dog*. Laurel was the star, Hardy just a bit player, and the association was so casual that, on the evidence of interviews they gave in the 'thirties,

Frames: Laurel, Hardy, James Finlayson and Tiny Sanford in Big Business.

both men forgot it entirely. Nevertheless they have an interesting scene together. Hardy in his usual role as a 'heavy' is holding up a man and taking his money. Laurel, passing by, stops just behind him, with the result that Hardy stuffs the money into Laurel's pocket. When he finds out, he turns his gun on him, and the first words spoken between them on screen are given in a title: 'Put 'em both up, Insect, Before I Comb your Hair with Lead'.

After training as a singer and running a cinema of his own, Hardy had been acting in films since 1913. In contrast to Laurel, who came into films as an established stage comedian, his roles were always subordinate ones: he made hundreds of films, of which little detailed record survives, and he continued working in this way after his fleeting association with Laurel. In the early 'twenties his most important work was for Larry Semon, the director/comedian. Then he signed a contract with Hal Roach, who was building up his Comedy All Stars team. Shortly after, in 1926, Roach signed Stan Laurel.

Since *Lucky Dog*, Laurel had never been absent from films for long. He had already made one series of films for Roach, and then a successful 'Stan Laurel Series' for another company. However, his interest was increasingly turning towards direction, and it was as a gagman and director that Roach now hired him.

In 1797 Coleridge spilt some scalding water over his leg, and therefore could not join his friends in a series of country walks. The result was the poem 'This Lime-Tree Bower my Prison'. In 1926 Hardy spilt scalding fat

Frame: early Laurel.

over his arm, and therefore had to cry off a Roach film, *Get 'em Young*, in which he had been cast as a butler. The result was no less important: the Laurel and Hardy partnership. What happened was that the accident forced Laurel, who had been set to direct the film, to take over the part himself. He was a success, and was persuaded to write himself into the next Roach comedy; by this time Hardy was fit again, so that the two men acted together. Laurel became reconciled to continuing as an actor (though he never, until forced to in 1940, gave up his close involvement in the writing,

direction and editing of the films), and within the framework of the Roach Comedy All Stars' work his *rapport* with Hardy grew.

In 1926 the biggest of Roach's stars was, marginally, James Finlayson. In a series of films, one can trace his gradual supersession by Laurel and Hardy. A Scot whose career is closely bound up with theirs, he had already filmed with both of them separately. In *Love 'em and Weep*, the first film to unite the three, Finlayson plays the lead, Laurel is his assistant at the office and Hardy has a small part as a guest at a dinner party; he and Laurel have no scene together. (When the film was remade in 1931 as *Chickens Come Home*, one of their weakest shorts, it was Hardy in the lead with Laurel still as assistant; Finlayson played the butler.)

In *With Love and Hisses* the balance is more even. Finlayson is a captain taking some part-time troops off to camp, by train. Hardy plays a sergeant, Laurel a private soldier. The format of the picture is much freer than the stagily plotted *Love 'em and Weep*, giving each

of them scope to use all kinds of individual 'business' developed over the years.

Laurel's hair is still smooth. But he already has what was to become his other chief trademark, his sudden collapse into weeping, the 'Laurel cry'. Though he claimed to have devised this in *Get 'em Young*, he had indisputably done so earlier, since he uses it in two at least of the Stan Laurel series of 1925, *Snow Hawk* and *Somewhere in Wrong*. He said also that this was one bit of business that

Frame: early Hardy.

he grew to dislike, but that Roach, when the Laurel and Hardy team became a success, persuaded him to go on using it. The impression one gets from the films is, rather, that the cry only found its true significance in the partnership with Hardy. It suits the 'child' role which he came deliberately to assume, and goes with all his other carefully-integrated symptoms of infant mentality. In this film, it is half-way there, a response to the bullying of first Finlayson, then Hardy. Laurel's name in the film, Cuthbert Lamb, is an index of his effeminacy, which is startling and goes far beyond anything in the later work. He has an extraordinary and brilliant scene in which, misinterpreting some parade-ground gestures of Finlayson, he persistently and to his growing fury makes eyes at him.

This pansy quality, exploited just as strongly in *Flying Elephants*, recurs after 1927 only, I think, in *The Midnight Patrol* (1933), and even then for a very brief moment; in many films he is to dress up as a woman, but these scenes have no homosexual overtones; in general, the effeminacy of Cuthbert Lamb becomes absorbed into the flat, asexual meekness of 'Stan'.

Hardy does his familiar 'heavy' characterisation, hair cut short, and looking tough, especially in a scene where, stripped to his singlet, he wolfs down a meal (surprisingly, in Laurel and Hardy films it is Stan who is keener on food). But within this stereotype he has developed promising bits of business. The truculent look and manner. The look of stoical resignation. The look of horror or apprehension (mouth forming an O) which he uses in innumerable early films for simple narrative purposes—reacting to a surprise and turning to run—but which is ready to become a powerful expression of *moral* shock.

Both the characters are 'there', but not yet quite realised. Laurel occasionally slips back into what is almost a Chaplin imitation (he was

12

once Chaplin's understudy). In this, and in other films of the series like *Do Detectives Think?*, it's as if they are marking time, waiting to join in a partnership where all their mannerisms will at once fall into place and each character be given edge by its special relation with the other. Already in *With Love and Hisses* there are scenes which foreshadow this relationship, Laurel's clumsiness causing trouble for Hardy. Good as the Finlayson/Laurel scenes are—and Finlayson is superb—they are not so rich in possibility.

Sugar Daddies is another film showing the three actors' relationship at a delicate stage. Finlayson again begins as the central figure, a millionaire trying to get out of an uncongenial marriage. Laurel is his lawyer (hair again sleek), Hardy his butler (hair centre-parted, as in *Love 'em and Weep*). The two soon contrive a scene on which a rich series of variations will be played in later films: Hardy, answering the door, has to struggle to get possession of a hat which Laurel is anxious to keep on his head. The main part of *Sugar Daddies* has Finlayson fleeing the bride's family by making Laurel ride on his back and be transformed by a coat and a wig into one very tall lady whose escort, and support, is Hardy. ('Who is this sunflower?' 'She's my little wife.') This is a stock farce situation used already in *Love 'em and Weep* and used inventively here; but there is an extra charge of significance in the way that Laurel climbs on Finlayson's shoulders, eclipsing him, to form a partnership, a 'marriage', with Hardy.

Hal Roach and his associate, Leo McCarey, were by now becoming aware of the potential of these two as a comedy team—as were cinema audiences. They decided to put them together into a new series of shorts, to be known as the Laurel and Hardy Comedies.

Frame: together in **Sugar Daddies.**

PUTTING PANTS ON PHILIP

Putting Pants on Philip was the first official Laurel and Hardy short to be made, though not the first to be released. They still don't use their own names. Hardy plays a highly respectable figure in small-town America, the Hon Piedmont Mumblethumber. He wears a boater. Laurel too is not yet his familiar self either in dress (kilt and tam o' shanter; he is Piedmont's nephew Philip come over from Scotland) or in temperament: the letter instructing Hardy to meet him off the boat had a postscript warning: 'Philip has but one weakness—women. At the sight of a pretty girl he has spots before the eyes. Guard him well.' Yet his sexual aggression goes together, oddly, with his later forms of timidity and dumbness. It is the dumbness which we see first, at the dock: he takes the immigration man's inspection of his hair for a personal assault and fights back; we also get his cry. The crowd jeers at him, none more heartily than Hardy, who says with particular enjoyment to this neighbour: 'Imagine—somebody has to meet *that*!' This prepares

for a fine, slow-motion Hardy change of expression in close-up. All it lacks is a despairing turn of the eyes towards the camera.

In town, Philip embarrasses his uncle by being conspicuous, and thus making *him* conspicuous. His chasing of women is not so much an offence in itself as a nuisance in drawing him out of Hardy's sight and thus, infallibly, into embarrassing situations. The kilt is what attracts the crowds, and it is used in the best tradition of the Donald McGill postcard, a vein of humour that is otherwise rare in Laurel and Hardy. Laurel stands above a grating, and a current of air blows his kilt up (as it does Marilyn Monroe's skirt in *The Seven Year Itch*). Hardy pushes him away angrily. While he pleads with the crowd to disperse, Laurel takes snuff, and as always he sneezes heavily—only this time he 'sneezes down' his underpants. Again he advances across the grating. Cut to the crowd watching: the females swoon, and are carried away by their menfolk. Hardy doesn't realise what's happened until a policeman comes up and complains 'This dame ain't got no lingerie on'. The incident makes him extra anxious each new time that Laurel evades him, which he does even at the tailor's where they have tried to 'put pants' (i.e. trousers) on him.

In this first half, Hardy has been not much more than a (very good) dignified foil to Laurel. Now their partnership begins to develop with greater speed. He hustles Laurel away from a new gathering of spectators and on to the top of a bus, determined to keep control of him. Laurel makes to sit down but Hardy, inaugurating a whole tradition of

self-important gestures, insists that *he* will take the spare seat. Soon, looking down into the street, he yet again sees people running in one direction (the crowd scenes are done throughout in a beautiful elliptical style, and the film, like most of their pre-1930 shorts, has the generous open-air 'breathing' quality that tended to get cramped by sound-film methods). He is reassured by seeing and grasping a kilt at eye-level. Still the flow of people continues; and it turns out that the kilt belongs to a different Scotsman.

Twice more, Hardy is to make trouble for himself by insisting on his own importance. He extracts Laurel from the new crowd; then the girl whom Laurel has been chasing passes them once more. Hardy forestalls him, and says *he* will go and chat her up. He advances in his best Southern-gentleman style, but is answered by a flick on the nose. Here we get the first true Hardy camera-look.

Laurel catches up with the girl as she is about to step off the pavement into a muddy street. He puts down his kilt, Raleigh style. (By now his underpants have been restored.) She steps deliberately over it. Hardy, having watched this snub, is doubled up with laughter —again, this is the first time of many, and, in line with the pattern of later films, retribution is not far off. He insists that *he* will step on the kilt, on his way across the road: so he steps on it, and through it, into the 5-foot-deep muddy pool which invariably lurks on the kerb, whether flanked by warning notices or—as here —not, as a punishment for complacency. Cue for the second true Hardy camera-look.

What has happened within this film can be plausibly read in terms of the two actors and their assumption of roles. Hardy starts as the elegant, dignified Southern gentleman, not far from his own status in real life. Laurel comes to join him from Britain. Laurel was, like Philip, the ladies' man of the pair, but in the course of the film he comes to abandon this role, a role symbolised by his little skip. At the end, the girl, after crossing the road without his help, looks back and does an affectionately mocking skip of her own: sexual initiative has been transferred from Laurel to women, and in the films this is how it stays. The skip was evidently an early Laurel trademark, like his cry: in *Flying Elephants* he even does it in extreme long-shot, which suggests it would be recognised by audiences. He uses it very occasionally in the later films when provoked into chasing someone, though never a woman:

in *Early to Bed* and *One Good Turn* when he chases Hardy, and in *Any Old Port* when he chases his opponent round the boxing ring. For his part, Hardy has grown from a passive figure to one who actively provokes his own fate and is ready to 'mix it' with Laurel and others. His camera-looks at the end announce a new relationship with the audience. (His first-ever camera-look was apparently improvised several films earlier, in *Why Girls Love Sailors*, but not till now has he found the ideal

use for it. The famous placatory 'tie-twiddle', also devised in the course of that film, has not yet become part of his repertoire.) Moreover: all through the film crowds have been gathering to look at Laurel (who has been a star for some time). At the end, with Hardy's definitive loss of dignity in the mudhole, the crowd gathers again, this time to stare at him. From now on, he will be as celebrated as his partner. This isn't of course to be taken as an allegorical meaning built in consciously like a cryptogram, but it exactly reflects the way things did work out. In *Battle of the Century* and *The Second*

Frames: Putting Pants on Philip.

Hundred Years they are already, quite simply, Laurel and Hardy.

At the start of every film they are already together, their familiar relationship is something 'given' and (except in one or two freak passages like the end of *Thicker than Water* and *A Chump at Oxford*) unchanging. For this reason, though they are occasionally given different names or, in the silents, no names at all, one is justified in referring to them from now on as Stan and Ollie.

A note on names

Stan changed his name from (Arthur) Stanley Jefferson to Stan Laurel in the course of his vaudeville career in America, before making his first film. In all his films he is thus billed as Stan Laurel.

Ollie was at first billed as Norvell Hardy or as Babe Hardy ('Babe' was a nickname dating from boyhood). After legally adopting the first name of Oliver, he was billed as Oliver 'Babe' Hardy, and later as Oliver N. Hardy. With Roach, he is plain Oliver Hardy.

In the sound films, he habitually introduces himself with dignity. 'I'm Mr Hardy— Oliver Norvell Hardy. And this is my friend, Mr Laurel'.

Supporting actors, too, generally keep their own names. Charley Hall is Mr Hall, James Finlayson is Finlayson or Finn, and so on.

Mr Hardy calls Mr Laurel Stan or Stanley. In *The Perfect Day* (1929, sound), his wife calls him Oliver; soon after comes this dialogue:
Stan—Step on it, Ollie.
Ollie—I'll step on you in a moment. And *don't* call me Ollie!
However, this is the only time he objects to the name.

Frames: getting the banana skin into position in From Soup to Nuts, *with Tiny Sanford and Dorothy Coburn.*

16

TECHNIQUES

The Laurel and Hardy Comedies were an instant popular success, creating a demand to which the studio responded. Leo McCarey says that he made at least 100 Laurel and Hardys up to 1930; even allowing for some loss of prints and records, the figure seems impossibly high, and it wouldn't be the only statement made by McCarey in this interview (*Cahiers du Cinéma* Feb. 1965) to be contradicted by other evidence. But the period 1928-30, covering the introduction of sound, was certainly the most prolific of their career, with an average rate of one 20-25 minute short in less than a month. The sustained invention of these films is astonishing. After 1930 they went on making several shorts a year, under the same conditions of creative independence, as well as the feature-length films which were becoming increasingly necessary for economic reasons and which set new problems of adjustment. The best of the mid-'thirties shorts are still very good.

The television critic of The Guardian, commenting on a recent showing of *Beau Chumps*, offered a generalisation about Laurel and Hardy which is still common:

'The amazing thing is how these films are still funny in spite of the lack of technical skill which makes them now seem gruesomely slow at times and almost always badly put together.'

To criticise Laurel and Hardy for their films' slowness is like saying Keaton is funny despite not having a very mobile face. In so far as one can isolate it, the 'technical skill' of Laurel and Hardy's shorts is comparable with Keaton's. The form of the films, and of the individual gags, is the ideal expression of their characters and their kind of humour: it has the only true criterion of artistic form, that of appropriateness or, better, necessity.

They were fortunate to have McCarey, one of the finest of all comedy directors, to help write and direct, or at least to supervise, their films up to late 1930. Within a few years of his association with them he made *Duck Soup* with

the Marx Brothers and won his first Oscar for *The Awful Truth* with Cary Grant and Irene Dunne. In their brief, intense collaboration, McCarey learnt his job, and Laurel and Hardy evolved a comedy form which was beautifully direct and at the same time deceptively subtle and flexible.

Consider first, as an exercise in comedy technique, the banana skin episode in one of the very early shorts, *From Soup to Nuts*.

Stan and Ollie have been sent along by an agency to wait at a private dinner party. A good idea, obviously, is for Ollie to fall face-down into a creamy gateau, but how is a banana skin to get into the right place? A lead-in gag (see illustrations) is devised which is delightful in itself (what manoeuvre, in fact, does Dorothy Coburn imagine her neighbour has been carrying out?) and functional in that when the banana skin is deposited, it comes as a natural next stage rather than as something arbitrarily contrived. The other essential is to get the most out of Ollie's deportment *before* the fall. While the dog eats the banana, Stan has been absently pouring soup over Ollie's shoe, and he reacts with righteous indignation. Now that he has the gateau, he is clearly going to show how to serve with

efficiency. The camera lingers on his face. No face can express self-assurance with greater economy.

The slow build-up conveys Ollie's ponderous complacency. At the same time it creates the kind of anticipation, as we foresee the fall but are made to wait for it, which doubles the laugh when it's eventually 'released'.

When Ollie lands in the cake he hardly moves, just looks up through a mask of cream. The deliberation of his 'slow burn' is part of his persona but, as in the earlier shots, the slowness has a 'technical' function, enabling the audience's laughter to be finished before the next action begins. This became an important part of their technique, solving the perennial problem which film comedy has to face in not being able to adjust its timing to the responses of each live audience: this can be particularly tiresome in dialogue comedy when laughter drowns whole lines. Stan would go with his collaborators to watch the new film with a preview audience, and adjust the length of some of Ollie's camera-looks in accordance with what was needed; sometimes, too, if a particular comedy routine went well they would extend it by further shooting. Only occasionally, as in the final sequence of *Leave 'em*

Laughing, does the result seem over-protracted when seen without a full audience. Occasionally, too, there is a jar when an incipient camera-look is cut off, presumably because the pace was thought to need tightening. As a rule the result is just ideally-timed comedy. The adjustment to an audience—whether physically there at a preview or, as must have become a habit, imagined—is not compromise but sensitivity. Watching in isolation, one still savours the extended camera-look because it *is* Ollie—which is what kept the audience laughing in the first place. In the slow build-up and the slow run-down, technique and content are indistinguishable.

In the silent films, they evolved a method combining planning with improvisation. Many of the routines, like Chaplin's, were made up as they went along, inspired by the situation they were starting from (building a house, waiting at table, playing golf, starting a car). However, form and structure are not loose. The principle of binding gags *together*—the banana skin 'justified' by the previous scene with the dog—is maintained. At best this makes for a delirious sense of inevitability in even the most outlandish actions.

Frames: From Soup to Nuts.

Already in *The Battle of the Century*, a film released before *Putting Pants on Philip* though made just after it, they have with deliberate bravado combined the two slapstick clichés of banana skin and pie-throwing. How can the pie-throwing convention be made fresh?— make the man with whom Stan and Ollie collide an employee of the Los Angeles Pie Company, carrying pies between the shop and his lorry. How can the banana skin device be used without cynicism?—build the plot deliberately around it. Ollie has taken out an insurance policy against injury to Stan, and is trying to collect on it in the way which occurs to him as easiest: making Stan slip on a banana skin. A series of miscalculations culminates in the pieman's falling on it. He naturally retaliates with a pie to Ollie's face. Ollie throws one back which misses and hits an innocent passer-by. With an unlimited supply of pies on hand, everyone who's hit can retaliate in kind: Stan assists by serving out pies from the back of the lorry. It is the first, if not the best, of their apocalyptic scenes of mass violence. Henry Miller (quoted by John McCabe) called it 'the greatest comic film ever made'. What I am stressing at this stage is the care in the overall planning (it is just this inevitability which is lacking in their disastrous, studio-dominated pictures of the 1940s). The most brilliant example of this is *Liberty* (1929).

Looking at a synopsis in advance, one might think the climax of *Liberty* impossibly contrived: Stan and Ollie stranded on top of a half-built skyscraper 'with Hardy suffering under the added disability of having a live crab in his pants' (*Monthly Film Bulletin*). Maybe they started from this idea and worked backwards, but if so it doesn't show, so rich and inevitable is the build-up. In many ways, Laurel and Hardy are a kind of comic equivalent of Hitchcock: the extraordinary

scene or image gains power from having its roots fixed in the ordinary. Plausibility on this level is a valid criterion for Laurel and Hardy's comedy, as it isn't for the Marx Brothers' or Tashlin's, because they are themselves so ordinary, corresponding to Hitchcock's often similarly complacent 'Everyman' figures. If their world wasn't seen to function by familiar rules of cause and effect, the outrageous situations they get into would lose their beauty. The films chart the way in which responses which are basically, in Raymond Durgnat's phrase, 'plodding and homely' can lead by their own power, not by the conventions of fantasy, to extraordinary situations.

Nothing happens in *Liberty* which is not completely logical. Stan and Ollie are in a getaway car, escaping from prison. Being chased, they have to pull their civilian clothes on hastily. Therefore they plausibly get the wrong trousers—but already they have had to hurry out of the car and into the street. Therefore they have to find a way of exchanging trousers in the street. Even now, the crab is kept in reserve for some time. In a beautifully varied succession of scenes they are surprised together in embarrassing postures,

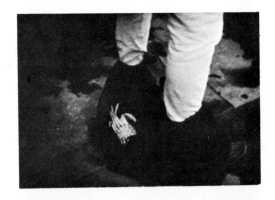

and have sheepishly to pull on the wrong trousers once more. Their fourth attempt takes them into an alley by a fishmonger's shop. The owner emerges suspiciously, again just before they have managed to swap. Stan knocks against a crate of fish, and a crab falls into the seat of his over-large trousers. Note that because the trousers are so large the crab can lie there undetected, which it couldn't were the trousers on Ollie. It only makes

Frames: The Battle of the Century (*opposite*), Liberty (*this page*).

21

itself felt when they are passing James Finlayson's record shop, still looking for a secluded corner; Stan makes a series of convulsive jumps forward, each causing new damage to Finlayson's stock, but the crab is lying so loose that still someone of Stan's dumbness can remain baffled. It remains for the film to get them, in this state, on to the skyscraper. Now that they have tried in vain so many spots for changing, one can't resent their turning to an apparently deserted building site. They undress—but a lift descends beside them and they have to go through the sheepish routine again

with the workmen, pulling on, still, the wrong trousers. The next stage is logically for them to find a more concealed spot, the lift itself. They actually exchange trousers this time, but while pulling his on with the crab inside Ollie leans back against a lever and the lift ascends. Puzzled by this, he doesn't finally do up his trousers till they are at the top. And it's entirely typical of them (a) that when they reach the top they should step out to see exactly where they are, (b) that when they realise, they should scurry back to the lift (but it's already been called to a lower storey), and (c) that when they see a ladder leading down from the girder opposite them they should not wait for the lift to return, but make their way round the structure in order to climb down. Since Ollie has only just got the trousers on, it's natural, rather than arbitrary, that the crab should begin to nip him when they are in the middle of the first precarious girder.

The whole skyscraper scene is superb, shot not only with exact timing but with such apparent authenticity as to communicate vertigo directly; but one can hardly overestimate the importance of a construction which makes the episode seem as probable, as normal, as anything in a neo-realist script.

Obviously it would be intolerable were I to go through all their films in this way. *Liberty* has the advantage of illustrating this aspect of their work with special purity. It goes in a very straight line, without much by-play *between* Stan and Ollie. One isn't aware at the time of the meticulous construction any more than one is aware of calculation in the timing of pauses; both these operate at the 'invisible' level of craftsmanship. Other silent films reveal other forms being developed, and reveal more of the subtleties of Stan and Ollie's characters.

Frames: Liberty.

STRUCTURE

The Finishing Touch was made in 1928, the year before *Liberty*. It's a remake of *Smithy* (1924), one of the Stan Laurel Comedies in which Stan played a builder and Finlayson his foreman, and it could easily, like *Smithy*, have been just a pleasant series of gags improvised from the situation 'building a house'. Stan repeats some of his business from the earlier film, and the climax is the same: the collapse of the house. The great advance is in the relation of gags to character, of which the last scene is a great illustration:

Stan and Ollie are contractors who get into an argument with a customer about the house he commissioned them to put the 'finishing touch' to. The two sides progress to throwing stones at each other. Having run out of stones, Stan and Ollie look round and see a nice big one, which they struggle to pick up—they even fight one another for it. They forget, however, that it is the stone which is keeping their own lorry steady on the slope above the house (we saw them fixing this at the start). When they remove it, the lorry rolls downhill and knocks the house flat.

As he realises what has happened, and as usual it takes a time to sink in, Stan drops the stone. It falls on Ollie's foot. Ollie jumps about in pain, picks up the stone, and throws it down on Stan's foot. All this, including the house's collapse, is in one shot, the last of the film.

The characters are expressed in action with a beautiful directness. Stan is dumb, Ollie impatient: all the subtle variations of their relationship, and they are many, are based on this distinction, which doesn't change. Every small-scale catastrophe in *The Finishing Touch* comes from some combination of dumbness and ill-judged violence. At the end, with perfect symmetry, violence (throwing stones) leads on to stupidity (picking up the brakestone) to destruction, then back to its origin in individual stupidity (Stan) and violence (Ollie)—the cycle might go on indefinitely.

The film still has less story-line than any other—even *From Soup to Nuts* has their progression from door to kitchen to table, and from one course to the next—and therefore shows them being compelled to work out a kind of comic form from within, not only relating gags to character but binding them together. There's something basically satisfying about a series of three (third time lucky, what I say three times must be true, etc) and one of the classic forms of 'the gag', analysed, is a triple one—gag, reversal, new reversal. In *The Finishing Touch* the form is, as yet, more diffuse than this, but it is still noticeable that things tend to happen three times. Ollie keeps trying to carry a door-frame up a ramp and on to the porch of the house. He has put a plank in position, to make a bridge between ramp and porch. The first time, Stan removes the plank just as he starts the walk—fall number one. The second time, Stan helpfully puts two halves of a plank on top of one thin plank, to strengthen it—result, fall number two. By now Ollie is wary and (after some intermediate action) insists on testing the next attempt at a bridge. It is firm: he looks confidently at the camera and strides across. When he gets across, the entire porch gives way under him.

what he is about to do; then straightens up, and bangs his head on the window-frame. The nails go down for the third time.

Each gag has been neatly rounded off, with Ollie suffering through no fault of Stan's: repetition would be anti-climax.

Likewise there are three humiliations for the nurse (the house is going up next to a hospital), three blows from projectiles and three other humiliations for the policeman, and so on. Many of their later shorts not only use this threefold structure of incident, but are made up of three roughly equal sections or episodes: five or six of their very best shorts come into this category. It was part of the difficulty of their transition to feature-length films that they went on using units of about the same length, 5-10 minutes, but had to put more of them together to fill the time, and the films, unless like *Sons of the Desert* very carefully plotted, lost their way: this applies particularly to their first two, *Pardon Us* and *Pack up your Troubles*, made at the peak of their career in sound shorts. The triple form both of gag and of short film, suited them ideally.

Films of the same year which have this triple structure are *Leave 'em Laughing* and *You're Darn Tootin'*.

I take the later film first. The title evidently means 'you're darn right'—the phrase is used by Stan in *Bonnie Scotland*—and is given point by their occupation as musicians: Ollie is a trumpeter.

(1) They disrupt their band and are sacked.
(2) At their lodgings.
(3) As street-musicians.

The three sections are, as always, linked: they lose their job, so cannot pay the rent, so have to play for money in the street. The first two parts are good and the last great. Like *The Battle of the Century*, it ends with a street-battle, but one much more firmly rooted in the

Later, he has to hammer some nails, and to save an extra journey puts a handful of them into his mouth. He misjudges a step down, falls, and swallows the nails (painful close-up).

He carefully puts down a box to make an extra step, and goes back for another mouthful of nails. Meanwhile Stan takes away the box for his own use. Ollie returns and falls—another painful close-up.

Next time (again the gag is not continuous) he gets everything right. Stan is out of the way. Before starting to hammer he leans out to show the policeman, who is standing outside,

relations between Stan and Ollie. It escalates from the first of the full-scale private battles between them, and it is this that makes it worth looking at in detail.

In their lodgings they have used a neat three-part gag which recurs later with variations (e.g. in *The Hoosegow*). They are sitting next to one another at dinner:
(1) Stan finds the salt-cellar is blocked, so he unscrews it, sprinkles salt on his soup, and

Frames: The Finishing Touch, *with Edgar Kennedy and Dorothy Coburn.*

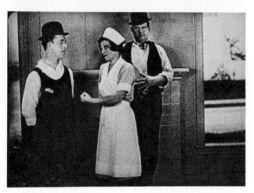

puts the top on without re-screwing it. Ollie reaches over for it—and shakes the whole contents into his soup. He looks grimly at the camera and exchanges plates with Stan.

(2) Unworried apparently by having heavily-salted soup, Stan goes through the same process with the pepper, and fails to re-screw it. Ollie thus pours all the pepper into his, formerly Stan's, soup.

(3) Stan reaches for the sauce bottle. Ollie snatches it and hides it under the table.

Like the end of *The Finishing Touch*, this is filmed in one shot to 'crystallise' their relation-ship. Both are slow to learn. Stan is dumb, but so is Ollie in making himself so vulnerable. Ollie is enraged but bears no lasting malice: his action in putting the sauce bottle out of reach is like that of an irritated parent protect-ing a child from its own clumsiness. And the fact of having him *remove* the bottle like this, unable to trust himself to combat Stan's carelessness even after forewarning, has a subtlety which explication could only labour but which is right at the root of Laurel and Hardy's genius.

So to the final section. When their playing

fails to charm money from passers-by, Ollie turns angrily on Stan and breaks his clarinet in pieces; though it's not apparent that Stan is any more to blame than he is. 'I wouldn't mind training a seal or an elephant, but you're hopeless.'

Stan retaliates by kicking his trumpet into the road. A truck narrowly misses it. Ollie turns indignantly to Stan to point out what he has nearly caused to happen. A second truck

Frames: The Finishing Touch *and (below)* You're Darn Tootin'.

passes and this time the trumpet is crushed flat. He wasn't warned by the first truck any more than by the salt-cellar; he also conveniently forgets who started the destruction. Outraged, he tilts his hat and comes purposefully 'through' the camera, always a sign that action is about to start. He walks up to Stan and hits him. Throughout this whole exchange they stay on the same strip of pavement and there is scarcely any cutting. The tempo is deliberate.

Hardy actions	Laurel actions
Hits Stan	Kicks Ollie
Hits	Kicks
Removes Stan's tie	Tears Ollie's tie
	Flicks his nose
Hits	Kicks
	Kicks
	Kicks
Tears Stan's hand-kerchief in strips	Removes Ollie's hand-kerchief to his own pocket
Hits	Kicks
	Kicks
Throws down Stan's hat	Throws down Ollie's hat
Stamps on hat	
Picks up the other	
Puts it on—it's too small	
	Picks up crushed hat
	Sees it isn't his
	Takes own hat from Ollie's head—smiles
Hits	Kicks
Hits	Kicks
Looks hard at Stan's waistcoat—rips it	Rips Ollie's jacket
Hits	Kicks

Stan thus wins, as he usually does: he gets in ten kicks to Ollie's left ankle, against seven of Ollie's blows to his ribs. He also keeps possession of a hat and a handkerchief.

Each time, Ollie has been moved to renew the assault by an injury to his property, an

injury to which he reacts with an expression of marvellously innocent outrage despite himself having injured Stan's property a moment before . . . . Both here and in the 'escalation' which follows, it doesn't strain the film at all to talk in terms of (unconscious) political fable.

Both give exceedingly vivid impressions of pain, Ollie hopping away each time with mouth open, Stan doubling up and clutching his ribs. Stan at least gets in a pre-emptive strike on three occasions but Ollie just keeps

Frames: You're Darn Tootin'.

coming back with the same tactics. In their early films such scenes as these, based on endless repetition, create an image of their relationship as something eternal, unchangeable, never modified by experience, which can't ultimately be enclosed by the finite form of the single or triple gag. The hitting and kicking ritual could go on for ever but is interrupted by a passer-by who speaks to Stan and thus seems, to Ollie, a potential enemy: so he hits him, and gets kicked back. This begins the escalation. The next man to appear is instantly kicked by Stan. More are drawn in.

Finding a man stationary in front of him, Stan pulls off his trousers. The man turns, misses Stan, and de-trousers someone else. The idea spreads. A stranger appears, wanders curiously into the mob of kicking, trouserless men, and soon gets the same treatment. A few moments later another stranger appears: this time the crowd doesn't wait but goes out to get him, leaping on him with communal frenzy. The war of all-against-all has developed a gravitational force of its own, sucking in neutrals.

Ollie is in the thick of things all along. Stan,

Frames: You're Darn Tootin'.

one of the last to lose his trousers, stands blankly on the same spot, the still point of a turning world, occasionally shrugging at the camera. Finally we cut away from the general chaos to a shot of a very fat, trouserless man: 'I've been robbed'. Cut to Stan and Ollie, trousered together, walking away, hats raised towards the camera.

An objector to the film and to Laurel and Hardy generally might compare them with Tom and Jerry of the MGM cartoon series.

30

After each clash they come back for more, without having changed or learned, just as Tom returns miraculously unscathed after extra-ordinary physical sufferings. Is this cartoon irresponsibility to be tolerated when the sufferers are human flesh and blood? But what in Tom and Jerry is a convention (itself an interesting one) is in Laurel and Hardy part of the theme. It is in their characters to be stupid enough, and tolerant enough, to wipe the slate clean after each encounter. They don't learn and they don't, for long, resent. But pain is by no means anaesthetised. Few actors suffer so vividly as (in particular) Ollie, or transfer their pain so fully to the audience. The films are highly therapeutic in letting us repeatedly indulge our violent urges but making us laugh at and judge them at the same time. They are the clearest illustration of the Aristotelian idea of purging. No one can like Laurel and Hardy without entering keenly into their marvellously direct kicks, punches, pokes in the eye, and other acts of violence; but who is inspired to emulate them in real life? Nor, like the violent heroes of certain gangster movies, do they get a token and delayed come-uppance at the end: when they are violent, retribution is decisive and painful.

However, this account of their violence and how it works is by no means comprehensive. When they walk off, re-united, the crowd is still in chaos: this 'infection' is significant. And the film is complemented by *Leave 'em Laughing*, which is constructed thus:

(1) In their lodgings. Stan has toothache. Various attempts to extract the tooth. Confrontation with the landlord.

(2) At the dentist's next morning. Ollie's tooth is extracted in error. In a rage, he tries to give Stan gas and pull the tooth himself for revenge. He succeeds in gassing both of them.

(3) In the street. Under the influence of

laughing gas they drive off and disrupt the whole traffic system.

It thus covers very neatly the three habitual levels of conflict in Laurel and Hardy (though these don't correspond exactly to the film's three sections):

Stan against Ollie

Both against a third party (landlord, traffic policeman)

Both against society (the traffic)

Some of the films work on just one level (*Early to Bed* and *Helpmates* on the first, *Big Business* on the second); most, as one would expect, oscillate between levels.

The last scene of many of the early films is a massive, intoxicating, social chaos. Besides the kicking and trouser-pulling in *You're Darn Tootin'*, there is the pie-throwing in *Battle of the Century*, the rice-throwing in *The Hoosegow*, the mud-throwing in *Should Married Men Go Home?* the boat-sinking in *Men of War*, and the traffic chaos in *Two Tars* and in *Leave 'em Laughing*. None of these films was made after 1930, which has led some commentators to regret a blurring of their Dionysiac force after this date. Only the army scenes in *Beau Chumps*, *Bonnie Scotland* and *Flying Deuces*, with their more conventional disruptions of military formation, are comparable. Their films do indeed change with the years; nevertheless, the disruptive force is implicit in their smaller-scale confrontations, it's not a special quality of the 'surreal' mass-chaos scene in itself. George Orwell wrote, in his essay on Donald McGill, that 'Whatever is funny is subversive': whether or not this is universally true, it is certainly true of McGill, Falstaff, and Laurel and Hardy. Falstaff is subversive in himself, not only when travestying the court or army. *Leave 'em Laughing* is subversive before the traffic jam has built up into a direct image of disruption. Other films are subversive without having any such scene.

The unrepressed violence of *You're Darn Tootin'* will already have indicated their way of being 'subversive'. The third section of *Leave 'em Laughing* starts with Ollie (who drives) pulling out from the kerb into the path of another car and bumping it. The driver leaps out and writes down their number in a notebook. They are hysterical with laughter and Ollie, in a gesture so quick as to be almost subliminal, *mimes* the man's act of writing as though in itself it were the most ludicrous action conceivable. We are not only made to jeer at the man's pedantic concern with justice: we are taken back by Ollie's gesture to a pre-writing stage of civilisation.

Doesn't this represent a classic subversive function of comedy—to take us back to our 'hunting' past where we can be as ruthless as we like with people and yet, because of the comic framework, avoid being 'Fascist'? (The violence in much of their work is too direct and cruel for one to invoke merely the safer word 'anarchic'; at least, if it wasn't comic it would be worse than anarchic.) It's much easier for comedy to have it both ways since we can more naturally feel both forces at once—the positive energy, blurred by 'civilisation', which we have to share; the destructive irresponsibility which we have to reject—without having to go through the more complex process of identifying with violence, then rejecting it as the forces of light close in on the hero . . . .

The pre-literate, 'hunting' past of the race has its equivalent in the ruthless solipsism of the child. Looked at another way, Stan and Ollie are children in dodgem-cars: this is what they evoke as they gleefully intercept or back into others.

The film is an extended playing not only of primitive violence against ordered society, but of childhood against maturity. There is the same balance here in our responses; we value maturity while liking to get back into childhood. This is the basis of Laurel and Hardy's comedy. Society is stronger if it takes account of primitive energies of which, in a sense, it is the denial; maturity is stronger if it doesn't cut itself off from the sharper childish drives which it by definition tames. All that Orwell, in the essay quoted, says of the Donald McGill postcards, can be applied to Laurel and Hardy. 'Like the music halls, they are a sort of saturnalia, a harmless rebellion against virtue.' They represent a less responsible man who 'is inside all of us, can never be suppressed altogether, and needs a hearing occasionally'. This, certainly, is Laurel and Hardy disrupting the traffic. But they go far deeper than McGill by giving us not only the 'static' other side of our responsible selves but the deeper roots of ourselves, from a time before the irresponsible and the responsible had to be separated. The dodgem-car violence of Laurel and Hardy— when they are drugged by laughing gas—is only one part of the very fluid and all-inclusive character which they build up from film to film, the key to which, as will be seen later in looking more analytically at them both in turn, is their childishness. 'The child is father to the man.'

It's not true at all of *Leave 'em Laughing* that 'the film ends as the entire street succumbs with him [the policeman] to paroxysms of pure delight' (McCabe). Everyone else remains stern and baffled. The policeman, in a thoroughly human detail, takes it out not so much on them as on the irate man whom they keep backing into. Finally he takes charge of their car himself and drives it into a muddy street where—as later in *The Perfect Day*—it sinks. The final image is of his bewilderment and of their still hysterical amusement.

Society (crowds) may be infected by their violence, but never by their laughter. Authority can't share their laughter here or at the end of *Scram* or *Big Business*. It makes itself absurd either by being laughed *at* or (as in *The Hoosegow*) by joining in the tit-for-tat violence. Stan and Ollie may even, having started a scene of chaos, blithely dissociate themselves, having proved that an anarchic force is latent in all of us, and all the better for being released once in a while—witness their new-found calm at the close of *You're Darn Tootin'*.

Frames: the last two shots of Leave 'em Laughing, *with Edgar Kennedy.*

GAGS

THE TRIPLE GAG

Some examples of the classic form of gag mentioned earlier, self-contained rather than, as in the looser structure of *The Finishing Touch*, spaced out; and more sharply pointed than the dinner-table routine in *You're Darn Tootin'*.

Early to Bed: Stan, working as a butler in Ollie's house, has been provoked into breaking the place up. Ollie tries desperately to stop him. He corners Stan, who is holding a precious vase, in front of a panel of three panes of glass.

Ollie throws a brick at him. It misses and goes through one of the panes.

Stan takes this in, thinks, and throws the vase through the second pane.

Ollie makes threatening gestures; Stan backs away frightened, knocks over a standard lamp, and the lamp goes through the third pane.

Busy Bodies: Ollie is sitting resignedly in the corner of the workshop, having been pushed there by Stan. Stan is helping him up when a workman asks him to put a jacket in the closet.

Stan opens the closet and the door hits Ollie in the face.

Ollie angrily bangs the door shut: the impact loosens a piece of metal that's hanging on the wall: it crashes down on Ollie's head.

Stan, returning, has to open the door again —it hits Ollie in the face.

One Good Turn. They are served a meal, out of charity, by a kind old woman. (A scene unique in their work. They have come to the door begging: this makes the scene of selfish violence that follows more than usually deplorable.)

Ollie picks up his cup and asks Stan for coffee. Stan, looking away, pours it to where he last saw the cup, which Ollie has now placed on the table. So the coffee goes over

Frame: the closet door in Busy Bodies.

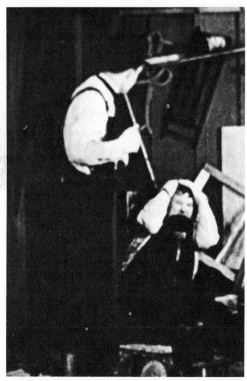

Ollie's trousers.

Ollie, with deliberation, pours sugar, and then the entire jug of cream, over Stan's trousers.

Stan caps this by adding coffee, spooning up the mixture, and flicking it into Ollie's face.

Way out West: They have been trying to lift Ollie up to a balcony by means of a pulley arrangement. He has crashed to the ground because of Stan's incompetence. Now they are each holding one end of the rope.

With cold premeditation, Ollie looks up, glances at the camera, and pulls viciously on his end of the rope, then releases it. Stan is lifted up and crashes down.

Ollie looks pleased but neglects to let go of the rope. Stan quickly recovers, pulls and lets go: Ollie crashes down. Stan looks pleased.

Ollie again prepares himself and pulls. But Stan, at the exact moment, throws wide his hands in his familiar look-it's-easy gesture. Ollie therefore pulls on nothing and falls. Stan's gesture is, brilliantly, at once the cause of his triumph and its celebration.

These scenes have all ended in humiliation for Ollie: they illustrate, with the conciseness of a limerick, the process in the films by which Ollie is undone by Stan's stupidity, his own stupidity, and Stan's shrewdness. The films are full of gags not quite so clear-cut, overlapping at one end or both into other bits of action.

One sequence is worth quoting which humiliates Stan and Ollie together.

Bacon Grabbers: They have been sent from the sheriff's office to claim Edgar Kennedy's radio because of his failure to pay instalments on it. Finally they succeed in collecting it from him.

Frames: Bacon Grabbers.

On their way off, they put it down in the road and pause. A steam roller comes along very slowly and crushes it. Kennedy is triumphant.

His wife (Jean Harlow) then appears with the good news that she has paid the outstanding sum, and the radio is theirs. Stan and Ollie triumphant.

The steam-roller continues on its course and crushes their car. End of the film.

THE OPEN-ENDED GAG

These are routines like the hitting and kicking ritual in *You're Darn Tootin'*, whose point is their repetition: they have no internal development but could go on for ever, giving an eternal image of Laurel and Hardy as though fixed in a circle of Dante's Hell.

They are commoner in the early films. We've already seen the fight in *You're Darn Tootin'*; the traffic chaos in *Leave 'em Laughing*, where Stan and Ollie's car is backed nine times into the car behind and their amusement is as strong and fresh the last time as the first; and the trouser-exchange in *Liberty* which never, until the skyscraper, gets any further advanced. There is a parallel to this last scene in *That's My Wife*, where Stan is made to dress up as Ollie's wife for an evening out. Some jewellery is dropped down Stan's dress and has to be retrieved: six times, Ollie is discovered in a compromising posture as he struggles uselessly to find it.

In one of the best of all the silent shorts, *Wrong Again*, they hear that a reward is being offered by a millionaire for the return of 'Blue Boy'. He means the painting, but they think he means the horse 'Blue Boy', and they take it round to his house. There they get the message to put it on the top of the piano. As Ollie, with his normal deference to authority says: 'It's his horse, and his house—we'll do as he says'. They contrive to get it there, and lean back against the piano to rest.

Thus, by a completely logical route Laurel and Hardy arrive at an image that irresistibly recalls the donkey on the piano in Buñuel and Dali's anti-logical *Un Chien Andalou*, made a few months previously, but no doubt unknown to anyone in the Roach studios.

The horse, a very well directed one, nuzzles Stan's hat from behind, tipping it slightly forward. Stan thinks it is Ollie and nudges him: Ollie smiles coyly, thinking the nudge is just a sign of friendship. Stan then tips Ollie's hat and he looks rather puzzled. The horse tips Stan's hat a second time. Stan retaliates harder against Ollie, who is startled. It happens a third time: Stan knocks Ollie's hat into his lap and is answered with angry words. Again they settle down. The horse tips Stan's hat and Stan impatiently knocks Ollie's to the ground. Ollie, retaliating for the first time, knocks Stan's to the ground and motions to him to pick up both. He does; they inevitably get the wrong hats; so when the horse tips Stan's a fifth time, he notices it's too big, looks round, and sees the horse. Without this, there is no reason why this triangular scene, filmed from in front in one lucid, intricately timed take, should ever have ended, since Stan and Ollie have each time returned to their original unsuspecting postures. As if to stress this, the next scene takes the idea even further.

After the re-exchange of hats, Ollie tells Stan to *sit* on the piano. He jumps up, but the addition of their combined weight to the horse's is too much and a piano leg gives way. Ollie kneels down to take the weight of the piano, and of the horse which is still on it, while Stan tries to fit the leg back.

The horse continues to take an interest in Stan's hat, and tips it off on to the floor. Stan leaves Ollie to bear the full weight again, and stoops to pick up the hat. He pulls up the piano, loses his hat again, drops the piano,

Frames: Wrong Again.

picks up his hat, lifts the piano, loses his hat . . .
the cycle is repeated a full seven times (in
another long, static take), creating the most
brilliant 'Inferno' vision in their work. Ollie
suffers agony each time. To Stan, Ollie's
agony and his own hatlessness are of exactly
equal weight, but even to say this is misleading
since Stan doesn't weigh them, which would
involve being aware of them simultaneously.
He is aware of them alternately. His failure
to absorb perceptions into any continuity

means he can never break out of the groove. It is the horse who tires first.

During all their complex manoeuvres with horse and piano, the owner is dressing upstairs. We see him from time to time, as he answers queries, or listens to the strange noises drifting up from below. There is a delightful sense of discontinuity between upstairs and below, not only in terms of what is happening but in time: we cut back to the owner after some strange protracted activity by Stan and Ollie, and all he has done meanwhile is put in a collar-stud. It's as if Stan and Ollie were in a separate time-continuum: it gives an effect as of the drowning man's quick visions, or of the lengthy dream lasting traditionally just a few moments of sleep.

It's like the scene already illustrated from *Big Business*, where the slow, dream-like alternation between Finlayson and Stan and Ollie—in 'subjective time'—is equal to one adjustment of his cap by the policeman in 'objective time'.

Though the truly visionary scenes of repetition, like this from *Wrong Again*, occur only in the silent films—and is there anything like them in the history of the cinema?—the principle is carried over into, for instance, *Any Old Port*, with its set-piece scene of Stan and Ollie signing the register in the boarding-house kept by Walter Long. Truffaut may perhaps be glancing at this in *Les 400 Coups* where the schoolboy starting an essay messes up successive pages of his exercise book. (there is more than one Laurel and Hardy allusion in Godard). Stan takes every imaginable chance of delay and ink-spilling. The action comes to a complete halt, signalled by the repeated close-ups of Walter Long glaring at them. In *Beau Chumps*, time stops when they try to pick up the right hats from the commandant's desk. The commandant stays expressionless at the corner of the frame

while they fumble, retreat and return as in some ballet. It may be this that the *Guardian* critic was thinking of as being 'gruesomely slow'. It could indeed be done quicker, or 'realistically' shortened; we'd then lose the crucial sense of Stan and Ollie being in and of the world but out of time with it. They and their directors are, I think, demonstrably sensitive to nuances of timing and cutting, even to the extent of slipping in little cinematic-time jokes like this (not unique) from *Helpmates*: Ollie is on the phone to Stan and tells him to come over right away. He puts down the phone and pauses a second or two; a ring comes at the door. He answers it and Stan is there. There has been no cut; Ollie looks startled; but they don't, happily, find it necessary to underline the joke any further.

Frame: Wrong Again.

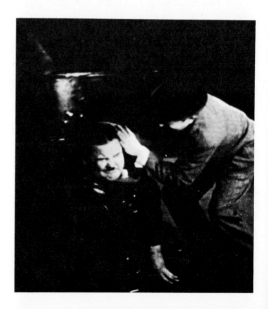

T E PERFECT D Y

The Perfect Day is one of the first Laurel and Hardy sound films. It shows them adjusting easily: in a positive way, using sound effects and dialogue wittily; in a negative way, not being inhibited by it. One needs to make no sharp separation between their silent and sound shorts.

Following their usual silent method, it was to a large extent improvised. It was Stan's policy always to shoot in sequence, so that he could control structure as well as tempo as they went along. *The Perfect Day* was planned as a three-part film: preparing a picnic, getting the car started, picnicking. But the second part inspired such a flow of gags that the third part didn't need to happen.

When Ollie, reacting to Stan's all-too-literal 'throwing-out' of the clutch, hits him on the head with it, we hear a resounding metallic clang. The constant background chatter of the wives and Uncle Edgar Kennedy, as they sit in the back seat waiting for the car to move off, is a delight. Apart from this the use of sound is very straightforward, giving us more economically what could, without altering the visuals much, have been conveyed by mime or titles. To hear, in these first shorts, cars, laughter, groans, music, and Stan and Ollie's voices (quite apart from what they say) is pure gain, and scarcely needs arguing at this stage in history, whatever Arnheim may have said about synchronous sound nearer the time. (The troubles of other actors at this period were due not so much to sound itself as to changing economic conditions in the industry. Laurel and Hardy began their career together at a later date than any other of the great silent comedians, and their still-growing popularity when sound came meant that there was no question of their doing anything else but go on turning out the old kind of films in the new conditions. Their art was at exactly that stage when they could most readily adapt themselves to a richer form. And being a team of two whose comedy grew out of their mutual relationship, they had an obvious need or at least use for dialogue, as distinct from sound effects, that solo comedians like Keaton and Chaplin didn't. *Men of War*, with its brilliant dialogue, shows how quickly they exploited the possibilities of the all-talking scene to go further into the two characters' psychology.)

The second point of interest in *The Perfect Day* is its control of tempo and the means by which this is achieved. Edgar Kennedy, the uncle, has a gouty foot which has kept him awake all night, but he's forced to come to the picnic with them. As we anticipate, violence is done to the foot—nine times.

It's rare for someone other than Stan or Ollie to suffer to this extent, except in a scene of reciprocal violence; the nearest equivalent is Kennedy's own suffering as the policeman in *The Finishing Touch*; since we don't feel for him what we do for them, it depends more than usually on sheer technique to get a laugh each time, which it does. John McCabe's long account of the film is admirably sensitive to its tone but inaccurate in detail, and the description he gives of the business with Kennedy's foot is somewhat misleading. He not only gets the spacing and frequency of the blows wrong, but attributes everything to the editing: 'They

39

come when they should come and this is determined in the cutting room'. This would be true if they were isolated gags which could be cut in anywhere. On the contrary, they are each time closely integrated into the total context, and their positioning is thus determined at the time of shooting. Only if the whole story were changed round could these gags' position be changed. In a film like this, the essential 'editing' has been done during preparation and shooting. Many gags, or even 'clusters' of gags, are filmed without cuts, and it needs emphasising that Stan and Ollie habitually deny themselves the chance of brushing up their timing in the cutting room at all: everything then depends upon their timing in performance. Even the technique of adjusting Ollie's camera-looks after a preview is limited in application, for many of them are contained within the shot (glance at camera and then away again) and are thus uncuttable.

Kennedy's gouty foot is each time seen in general shot. We watch the action closing in upon it.

(1) While Stan and Ollie prepare the sandwiches, he sits on the sofa with his foot up, holding a cane which he later uses to try to keep people out of range. Trying to avoid the picnic, he argues with Mrs Hardy, and to emphasise his point brings the cane down decisively—on his foot. This is just a prologue.

(2) Stan is sent by Ollie to fetch a chair. He pulls away the one on which Kennedy's foot is resting. The foot falls on to a dog sitting under the chair: the dog retaliates by biting it and refusing to let go. Only when it has all happened in general shot do we cut closer to a shot of dog and foot.

(3 and 4) Outside: Kennedy, in the back seat, puts his foot up along the side of the car. Ollie is in the driver's seat. Stan, from outside, shuts the door hard on Kennedy's foot. He

yells; Ollie remonstrates with Stan and leans back to strike at him with his hat—he misses and strikes the foot. All this in one shot.

(5 to 8) This sequence too—a true 'gag-cluster'—is done in one static shot. The car has a puncture. To reach the tools, they have to move Kennedy from the back seat and sit him on the running board. Ollie stands behind the car and tells Stan to pass out the jack: to get it, he removes the back seat and dumps it painfully on Ollie's fingers. Ollie shuts the door in order to get at the wheel: Stan opens it again, banging Ollie's head (two gags already, then, in this take before the gouty foot is involved at all). Ollie angrily tells him to come down from there and brings the jack. He steps out and treads on Kennedy's leg, Kennedy yells, Ollie makes an aggressive gesture at Stan, who drops the jack—on Kennedy's foot. He yells and takes the precaution of moving his foot from ground to running-board. Stan is now stumbling away from Ollie's anger and sits down hard on the running-board: another yell from Kennedy who then shifts his foot further out of range—only to have the door shut firmly on it by Stan. The only interruption to this superb and gruelling sequence has been a brief cut-in of Kennedy laughing at Stan and Ollie's clumsiness, just before Stan treads on him. Never, even for laughter of Ollie's, was punishment swifter or more decisive.

(9) Like the first blow, this is his own fault. They are making slow progress in changing the tyre. Kennedy gives Stan some instructions about how to free the punctured one. He stands very close: and, as we have foreseen for some seconds, the wheel itself, with the full weight of the car, crashes on to his foot. It is the longest and most excruciating pain of all and he has to endure it until Ollie can jack up the car and release him (which he does with striking efficiency).

After this, any more violence against him

would be anti-climax. He fades into the background, where he obsessively guards his foot and is jeered at for his caution by the two women.

Notice how beautifully the pattern has built up: from one impact (his own fault) to 1½ (the foot hitting the dog is presumably rather painful, as well as the bite) to 2 to 4 to one sustained impact (his own fault): then a slow fade-away.

Once shot, none of these gags, except possibly 1 and 2, could have been cut or changed at all without causing a hiatus in the visuals and/or the narrative. Removing even 1 or 2 would create loose ends. The only concession to conventional 'cutting-room' comedy technique is the insert shot of Kennedy before blow 5.

I'm not suggesting that all other comedians create their gags in the cutting-room, nor that there has to be anything wrong in such a technique: all the scenes of mass-violence in Laurel and Hardy are necessarily done, in part, this way. It's equally true that some scenes in *The Perfect Day* are formed by editing: the brief tit-for-tat scene with the neighbours (on which McCabe is excellent), and the repeated scenes, punctuating the action, in which they exchange long good-byes with the same neighbours. But these aren't quite the same kind of gag.

One can't leave the topic without detailing another scene, from near the beginning. Stan and Ollie, having made the picnic lunch, are all smiles. Ollie, who is holding the tray, drops a sandwich, and politely asks Stan if he will pick it up. To get at it, he has to push the door to (they've just come through the door from kitchen to living-room). He bends, the door swings *back* and hits him behind, he stumbles forward and butts Ollie in the stomach. Ollie drops the tray and it rests on Stan's back. After a momentary pause,

Stan straightens up, looking blank: the sandwiches crash to the ground. Ollie reacts angrily and a fight begins .... It is as brilliant a piece of 'physical' business as anything in their work, perhaps in anyone's work: it's in one shot, and couldn't be otherwise, since half the pleasure comes from *seeing*, thus knowing, that the intricate mechanics of it are all genuine.

The same is true of this no-cutting scene from *Our Wife*, 1931: Ollie, dressing excitedly for his wedding, has just put on his trousers. He walks away from the dressing-table, and the braces—buttoned only at the back—trail behind him. At this moment Stan enters, picks up something from the dressing-table (there's a sound of cloth tearing) and goes straight out. Ollie doesn't react; but in the next scene he is, without realising it, trouserless.

Stock comedy technique: shot of foot treading on braces, shot of trousers tearing ....

Frame: final shot of The Perfect Day.

THE HOOSEGOW

Neither Mr. Laurel nor Mr. Hardy had any thoughts of doing wrong — —

As a matter of fact, they had no thoughts of any kind — —

The Hoosegow, made in the same year, provides an ideal companion to *The Perfect Day* for detailed illustration, having a more complex, less improvised plot, and relying more upon editing in ordering its different kind of material.

The year 1929, containing as it does *Liberty*, *Wrong Again*, *Big Business*, *Bacon Grabbers*, *Angora Love* and *Men of War*, as well as these two, is unquestionably the richest of their career.

Hoosegow is slang for prison. The film has three parts:
(1) Their arrival at the prison building.
(2) As prison-camp labourers.
(3) A rice-throwing fight with the Governor and his entourage.
As in *Liberty*, much of the exhilaration comes from the *logic* with which the story moves to a fantastic ending.

When they reach prison they have a prolonged encounter with the warder, culminating in an abortive bid to escape. They are meant to throw an apple over the prison wall as a signal for a rope ladder to be let down for them. The apple which Ollie holds in readiness is detected by the warder and taken. Stan hides his in his mouth and suffers agonies trying to extract it, then contrives to swallow it. Ollie shows us he has a second apple, but his over-confidence gets that confiscated too. The warder, now exasperated, throws it right out of the prison. The plot now moves with unusual swiftness. Though the film has sound, not much is lost in the silent version which one sometimes encounters; and it translates well into a strip-cartoon layout, as here:

Frames: The Hoosegow, *with Tiny Sanford as the warder. After the attempted jail-break, Stan and Ollie are locked out when he goes back to fetch his gun.*

Next, we fade in on a prison-camp, with Stan and Ollie in the middle of a line of men digging a trench.

The little scene that develops with Stan, Ollie and pickaxes fixes their relationship as satisfyingly as anything in the earlier films. To define Laurel and Hardy for someone who's never seen them, show him this.

Stan is dumb to hit him, Ollie is dumb to make himself so vulnerable. Both are dumber to let it happen again, with the pick getting caught in Ollie's jacket. Stan is incapable of pulling it out the way it went in. Ollie is now so enraged that he blindly pulls at it, causing a great rip.

Ollie is later to lose more of his jacket the same way, and to have his hat pierced. But now, his rage is interrupted by the passing of a warder: he resumes digging with characteristically hypocritical keenness.

When the triangle is struck for lunch, Stan, always slow to interpret symbols, wonders what it is. When he's told, he sprints instantly

provides 'grounding' for the final section to come: the governor's arrival doesn't seem arbitrary when we've had a hint about it in advance.

Now that the warder turns them off, Stan and Ollie have to ask about food at the cookhouse. They are told to chop some wood and bring it in; then they can eat. The more wood the more food. The limit of Stan's ambition is a small twig which he picks up proudly. Ollie is scornful and addresses himself to a full-grown tree. Once again, there is scope for some exhilarating by-play between the two: Stan keeps undermining Ollie's dignity, or getting in the way, and is chased off by an Ollie whose deterrent is to take off his hat and brandish it. As soon as Stan halts and gestures back at him, he runs away in turn. It's one of the simplest of their films, in content. Eventually Ollie does fell the tree. As it begins to topple, an elaborate crane shot takes us vertically up the trunk and a snore is heard. The tree has the camp look-out post at the top: as the guard wakes, screams, and falls with the tree, we can see that it's Charley Hall. From this point—at which, incredibly, the French and Italian versions of *The Hoosegow* end—the film really takes off.

towards food; his 'instinctual' drive for food often compares with Harpo's for food and women, pure libido. Ollie trips in the trench, and they are both late arriving. The tables are full. One of the convicts points to a separate table for two and says it's for them. This is an occasion where Ollie, who in *Tit for Tat* is to baffle Stan with his own sarcasm, is deceived along with him. They settle down at the table. On this their first day in prison, they behave as they are accustomed to. They live in the present moment, looking neither before nor after, their morale conditioned by their immediate environment. So they respond as they always do to a well-stocked table, with relish. Stan unscrews the pepper, tips a pile into his palm, sprinkles an appropriate pinch of it over his soup, tips the rest of the pile from his palm into (yes) the soup. . . . Ollie takes the pepper, tips it up, and, the top being unscrewed as in *Leave 'em Laughing*, it all goes in. Coldly angry, he pours the soup on the ground. It splashes on a shoe, the shoe of the warder who is now standing over them.

He had been called away from his table by a message saying the governor is on the 'phone. His absence thus at the same time makes possible Stan and Ollie's scene at the table, and

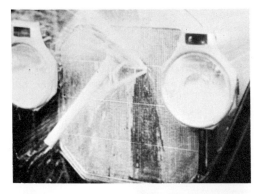

The tree falls right across the camp tents. People rush to see what has happened. At this moment, Governor Finlayson arrives at the head of a fleet of limousines. Everyone sprints back again to resume his occupation. The Governor's inspection, mercifully remote from Stan and Ollie, is itself a delight. He struts around the camp, seeing nothing; but when, passing a tent, he has his top hat knocked off by one supporting rope and stumbles on another, this is something he can understand: 'Have that seen to will you, Sanford?' 'I will indeed Sir.' This gains from being done cursorily in long-shot, a throwaway piece of satirical observation; most of the time we are back with Stan and Ollie at the trenches. Quite unaffected by what they've been through since they left here last, they are going through the same routine with the pickaxe. In a fit of rage, Ollie throws Stan's lethal weapon right away. He turns to resume—but a crash is heard and he looks round. The pickaxe has pierced the radiator of the leading limousine and water is spurting out. They approach it fearfully and wonder what to do, but are saved (as at lunch) by a fellow-convict's advice—fill it with rice. It seems a good idea, they fetch rice from the cookhouse: the flow

of water does indeed stop.   They put back the top hastily and return complacently to their posts as the Governor and party return. Finlayson is saying knowledgeably to the warder, in spite of the tree lying across the camp 'Well, everything seems to be quite in order'.   They all get into the cars and prepare to go.

When, after some revving, 'cooked' rice begins to spurt from the radiator, people start to notice: the chauffeur, Finlayson (with a convulsive stare), Stan and Ollie, and the warder, who may not know how it happened but

can guess who is responsible.   He calls Stan over and pushes him hard, so that he falls, face down, into what is now a large pool of rice.

Everyone watches Stan, immobile.   Slowly he picks himself up, scoops up some rice, looks at the warder, and pauses.

Frames (next three pages): The Hoosegow—details of the escalation, which ends soon after in a free-for-all.

On next spread, read across double page from left to right.

STAN

Their First Mistake (1932) is a film about the Stan Laurel character.

Their 'mistake' is in getting a baby. The film ends abruptly, and might seem at first sight a minor, low-pressure one, like others of the domestic series (*Be Big*, *Chickens Come Home*)—a variation on the old boys-versus-wives formula perpetuated in a hundred strip-cartoons.

A number of the films, starting with *Their Purple Moment* (1928), give wives to both of them. In *Blotto* (1930) only Stan is married, and in *Their First Mistake* only Ollie: this pattern recurs, whereas the *Blotto* one doesn't. The conflict between domesticity and irresponsibility is more meaningfully centred on Ollie.

The underlying pattern is normally the same whether Stan is married or not: Ollie wants to evade the wife or wives and go out with Stan. Even in *The Perfect Day*, where the wives aren't so important, there is a continual conflict between their decorum and the husbands' outbreaks of violence, and Ollie himself fluctuates between a sickly sharing of their picnic-in-the-country cosiness and bursts of angry energy which the wives have to fight: 'Boys, boys, enough of this foolishness!'

Mrs Hardy—played over the years by several different actresses, most memorably by Mae Busch and Daphne Pollard—is on the side of financial security, a good job, and a well-ordered home. In *Sons of the Desert*, where Ollie asks if he can go to an all-male convention with Stan, she is in favour of 'a nice resort where they play bridge and have lectures on art'.

With all such ideals, the very presence of Stan is incompatible. *Their First Mistake* looks more closely than the other shorts at what 'going out with Stan' involves.

The familiar triangle situation is established at the start, with some sharpness. Mrs Hardy (Mae Busch) nags at Ollie to get on in his business and not waste time with Stan. At this moment, Stan rings to ask what he's doing in the evening. Ollie, accepting the date, cunningly makes out to his wife that it's his boss, 'Mr Jones', inviting him to a business get-together; but Stan, at the other end, can't grasp what Ollie could mean when he keeps saying 'Mr Jones' down the phone with such emphasis. After some puzzled checking on his own identity, he goes round to the Hardy's to put Ollie right. Mrs Hardy's pride turns to active disgust, and they have to take refuge in the bedroom.

Frames: Their First Mistake, with (opposite) Mae Busch as Mrs Hardy.

There follows a dialogue scene lasting over two minutes, taken in one static medium shot. They loll together on the bed. Their timing is as admirable here as in the intricate physical manoeuvres of *The Perfect Day*. The dialogue, though it gets its full force only when one can mentally recreate the movements and intonations of the actors, bears transcribing in full:

Laurel (who has just witnessed Ollie being beaten, and shouted at, by his wife): Did you ask her about going out tonight?
Hardy: (nods)
L: What did she say?
H: You heard what she said!
L: Well, what's the matter with her anyway?
H: Oh, I don't know.
She says that I think more of you than I do of her.
L: Well you do, don't you?
H: We won't go into *that*.
L: You know what the whole trouble is?
H: What?
L: What you need is a baby in your house.
H: Well, what's that got to do with it?
L: Well if you had a baby . . . and it would keep your wife's mind occupied . . . you could go out nights with me . . . and she'd never think anything about it. All your troubles

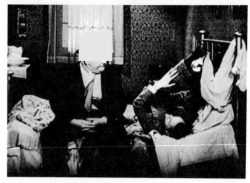

would be over ... Wouldn't think a thing about it.

H: You know, I think that's a pretty good idea.

L: You bet your life it's a good idea.
You know, it's a well-known fact ... that all the happiness in the house ... when you have a baby ... and there's a wife, and you, and the baby ... it's a well-known fact.
I know, I've read about *that.*

H: I'm beginning to think that you're right.

L: You bet your life I'm right. You know, I'm not as dumb as you look.

H: You bet your life you're not. Anybody that could think—
What do you mean, you're not as dumb as *I* look?

L: Well—

H: Come on!

L: Where are you going?

H: We're going to adopt a baby. Come on.

L: What for?
(Ollie drags him off.)

During the scene, Stan lets his legs climb idly over the head of the bed, toying around with things in the manner of a gauche adolescent. His illusory knowingness and his 'butterfly' mind fit in with this.

Stan as adolescent soon gives place to Stan as 'other woman', pushing further the implications of 'We won't go into that'. They come back from the adoption people with a baby for Mrs Hardy, but find out that she has already walked out and set the law on them. A process-server hands divorce papers to Ollie, and to Stan a summons for 'alienation of Mr Hardy's affections.'

Next, a scene with Stan as 'father'. Ollie, left holding the baby, calls him back plaintively when he tries to sneak off. The scene is played with a parody emphasis which is

slightly excessive, good though the idea is of having Ollie acting like an unmarried mother. Stan finally makes for the door but is caught. We now cut to the pair of them in their night shirts, getting the baby settled down. With the plot element behind them, they are starting from scratch, two men and a baby. In this situation, Stan finds a new role, that of 'mother.' Undertaking the task of feeding the baby, he slowly, to a crescendo of scandalised camera-

Frames: Their First Mistake, *with Billy Gilbert as the process-server.*

looks from Ollie, unbuttons the top of his nightshirt—then brings out a baby's bottle which he has been 'keeping warm'.

After certain diversions, they end up all together in bed. Ollie is wakened by the baby's cry, and sleepily holds a bottle across. The noise stops. But it happens to be Stan lying next to him. There is an agonisingly protracted sequence as Stan instinctively locates the teat, sucks, and goes on sucking. He has got through a bottle and a half plus one rubber teat before Ollie realises. He registers exasperation, and the film ends.

The end is perfect because the film, having tried Stan as adolescent, lover, father and mother—each time a 'mate' for Ollie—has settled on his true role, that of baby.

It's not uncommon for the Laurel and Hardy relationship, like that of Batman and Robin, to be taken as one of veiled homosexuality, and the script of *Their First Mistake* is certainly more suggestive than would be possible in an 'innocent' cause today, especially when two men are sharing a bed (as Stan and Ollie invariably do). 'She says I think more of you than I do of her'. 'Well you do, don't you?' 'We won't go into that'. The writ served on Stan for 'alienation of Mr

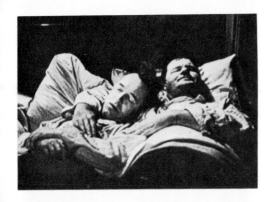

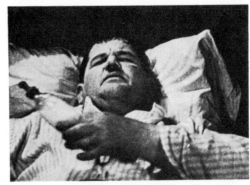

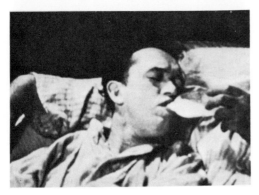

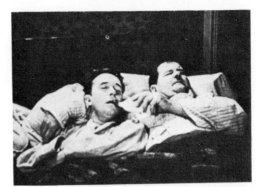

Hardy's affections' suggests a comic equivalent of the Maughams and Gerald Haxton; André S. Labarthe wrote that *Liberty*, with its repeated discovery of Stan and Ollie in a state of undress, 'offers, to anyone who can read, the unequivocal sign of an unnatural love'. There is something rather absurd about discussing this seriously at all, but *Their First Mistake* surely gives, to anyone who can read, an explicit rebuttal of Labarthe, though one which only confirms the evidence of all the other

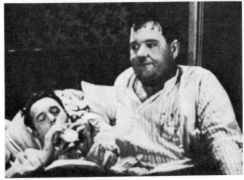

Frames: Their First Mistake.

films. Laurel and Hardy's world is pre-sexual, a nursery world. It can in turn be argued that there is no such state really as the pre-sexual, that homosexuality itself consists of a fixation at a certain level of immaturity, but this isn't to establish much, for there is so much that is childish about Laurel and Hardy that their sexual 'backwardness' is consistent with their psychic age, therefore natural. Since their mental processes, particularly Stan's, are those of nursery children, one takes it for granted that they should share a bed as in the nursery.

Ollie acts as foil for Stan in this film but to some extent the 'baby' definition applies to him too. Often when he plays the grown-up to Stan's 'baby', that is just what he is doing: *playing* grown-up. He treats his wives, in various films, the way a child acts marriage in play, with sloppy little blown-kisses and simperings. (In *Thicker than Water*, when he kisses his finger and coyly extends it to his wife's lips, she joins in the game and bites it hard.) The same with jobs: his 'Mr Jones' act is like a child playing telephones. In a

Frames: Daphne Pollard as Mrs Hardy in Thicker than Water; *and (opposite)* Beau Chumps.

very early film, *The Second Hundred Years*, they escape together from prison disguised as painters, and to allay the suspicion of a policeman they 'paint'—i.e. they brush white paint liberally over everything in sight, cars, shop-fronts, pavement, in the earnest, pre-occupied manner of a child who announces 'I'm a painter'. Everyone who writes about Laurel and Hardy is brought to focus on their childlike qualities: their innocence, their forgetfulness, their squabbling, and at the root of everything their logic.

They are a pair of overgrown babies who, in Freudian terms, have not grasped the 'reality principle': they have not learned to separate their own ego from the outside world. More than once this is illustrated in extraordinary episodes which are close to the terms used by Freud himself in discussing the way infants have to learn to sort out where sensual gratifications come from. In *Angora Love*, and again in *Beau Chumps*, Ollie comes indoors with aching feet, sits down on the bed alongside Stan, unwittingly takes off Stan's boot instead of his own, and massages the foot. It is taken further in *Beau Chumps*, the later film: he rubs the foot all over and blows delicately between the toes, and since the film has sound we also get his ecstatic sighs and 'Oh, that feels so *good*'. In *A Chump at Oxford*, a concealed joker adds a hand of his own to those of Stan, who is sitting on a bench, and Stan accepts it and 'feels' with it. Stan in particular has difficulty in ordering the perceptions which come to him through different senses. At the start of *Beau Chumps* he reads out to Ollie a letter which contains bad news. When Ollie reacts to it he asks what the matter is. 'Well, you read it, didn't you?'. 'Yes, but I didn't listen'. In *Helpmates*, he is telling Ollie how he was bitten by a dog; Ollie asks where it bit him and he responds by lowering the mouthpiece to

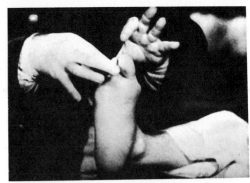

his leg to 'show' him. Neatest of all is an incident towards the end of *Their First Mistake*, i.e. just before Stan finally labels himself as an infant. They are trying to get the (other) baby to sleep, and Ollie insists 'If you must make a noise, make it quietly'. Stan puts in some earplugs, explaining that if he does make a noise he now won't have to hear it. This in itself earns a massive double-take from Ollie; the earplug detail, like so many things in the careful structure of their films, is then forgotten for a time but kept in reserve. When Stan has to move a standard lamp up close to

Twenty—Ollie, with some smugness, calls out Twenty-One, but when the count reaches Stan there is silence. Ollie repeats Twenty-One: still no response. The officer asks Stan impatiently 'What's your number?' and Stan, puzzled, tells him his Hollywood phone number. (He never gets the hang of numbers at all. In *The Midnight Patrol* their police car receives a radio message 'Calling car thirteen, calling car one-three'. Stan to Ollie: 'I though he said car thirteen'.)

Stan is like a child who is still learning by imitation and can't grasp abstractions or make

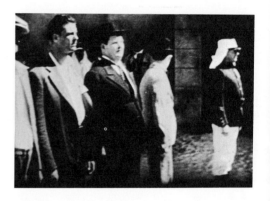

the bed, the flex won't reach and he has to find a new socket. (Meanwhile, Ollie has been spectacularly tripped by the taut flex.) The only one accessible is just outside the window, where a lit-up sign indicates ROOMS. Stan plugs in the lamp to an empty socket, but without noticing that the sign is set to flash rhythmically on and off. Naturally, when he gets inside, the lamp keeps going off suddenly. This gives him scope for one of his finest solo scenes as he struggles despairingly to relate cause and effect. One of his inspirations is to take the earplugs out and see if *that* stops the lamp from pulsating. The fact that this is so unforced and incidental—even missable—on the screen, is a good illustration of the richness of their best shorts, of which *Their First Mistake* is undoubtedly one.

Stan's mental processes have an inexhaustible interest. His behaviour is based on a child's failure to make connections, or the right connections; he cannot synthesise, and his 'memory' isn't much more than a set of conditioned reflexes.

Beau Chumps provides a 'diagram' of his inability to extrapolate. The camera tracks smoothly down the ranks as the new recruits to the Foreign Legion number off. Nineteen—

any jump in reasoning. Ollie's attempts to communicate by gesture fail unless they are completely explicit. When, in *The Music Box*, he points to the piano, and to the top of the slope, and then nods decisively, Stan can grasp what he means, and helps lift it; but when in *Scram* they have urgently to climb through a high window, and Ollie bends down for Stan to climb on his back, the inference is too difficult: Stan kneels beside him. In *Angora Love* they have a goat in their lodgings which the landlord mustn't know about. When he is heard approaching, Ollie looks for a hiding place while Stan holds the goat. Ollie lifts up the bed and points—Stan leaves the goat and scrambles underneath.

In *Our Wife*, Ollie, thanks to Stan's tampering, mistakes fly-killer for mouthspray. His cries of agony bring in Stan, and to show what's happened he points angrily at the flyspray and at his mouth. Stan helpfully picks up the can and begins to spray him.

Later in *Angora Love*, they are giving the goat a bath when a knock comes at the door. To make things look innocent for the landlord, Ollie takes out the goat and hides it, plunging Stan's head into the soapy water in its place. In fact it is only a fellow-lodger who has got the wrong room. Stan is rather baffled by this operation but like a curious child he manages to learn from it and put his experience into practice. They are engaged in washing the goat again when the landlord himself arrives and enters without knocking. Stan eventually looks up and sees him watching them, whereupon he instantly throws out the goat, thrusts in Ollie's head, and soaps it. Again, the unobtrusiveness of this, in its context, is striking. Ollie, furious, struggles out of the basin and hurls its contents at Stan —he ducks and they go over the landlord. We are at once absorbed into a classic, slow water-throwing routine; Stan's beautiful illogicality is not lingered on with any hint of self-congratulation, while the water-throwing climax in turn has been carefully grounded, so that there's no feeling of a contrived set-piece. It's the banana-skin law of *From Soup to Nuts*, extended.

Laughing Gravy has a virtual remake of this scene, with a dog instead of the goat, and there is something similar in *Come Clean*, and in *Way out West*—a comparatively late film, but Stan doesn't change. Ollie, somehow, has had a trap-door broken over his head in such a way that his head protrudes, very vulnerable,

Frames: Way out West *and* (*opposite*) Their First Mistake *and* Beau Chumps.

at floor level of the room above. Stan tries in vain to pull or push his head through; then their enemy (Finlayson) is heard approaching. Stan puts an inverted bucket over Ollie's head, intelligently; next, he sits on this bucket and *puts another bucket over his own head.*

Stan has a literal mind: he cannot grasp metaphor, or hidden complexities. When he accidentally slices through a phone cable, in *The Midnight Patrol*, his remedy is to tie the two ends together. In *The Hoosegow*, he and Ollie are trying to escape from prison: the warder detects their accomplices outside the wall and rushes out through the gate to try and catch them. Stan and Ollie follow him out and are thus free. The gates shut behind them. But Stan has a fixed, single response to the situation 'being shut out', and at once knocks loudly on the door. (If ever, as in *Night Owls*, they're trying to break into a house and Stan finds himself faced by the front door, he has a disastrous tendency to ring the bell.) In *Laughing Gravy*, Ollie has gone outside on a freezing night (unknown to the landlord, once again their enemy) to fetch in their eponymous dog. Stan is meant to be hauling them both up, on a rope of sheets, to their first-floor window. He first pulls up the dog and settles him down inside the room. There is a shot of Ollie below, and then a shot of Stan sitting with the dog by the open window. Now that they are in separate shots, Ollie doesn't impinge on Stan's mind: it is almost a rule that his world is only what is encompassed, at each moment, by the frame. Form = content. He is now just a man sitting in front of an open window on a cold night, so what more natural than to close the window?

In *The Bohemian Girl* Ollie puts his foster-child to bed, while Stan watches benignly. Ollie tiptoes away, enjoining silence, and draws a curtain across. They sit down. Now that the child is out of the frame she is out of Stan's consciousness, and since he has nothing to do he at once starts singing loudly. . .

The transition to sound naturally gave Stan extra scope.

One of the finest scenes in all Laurel and Hardy is the middle part of the three-scene short *Men of War* (1929). Stan and Ollie are taking two girls to a soda fountain but have

only 15 cents, which Ollie calculates will buy three drinks: so he instructs Stan 'When I ask you to have a drink, you refuse' (the possibility of Ollie making the sacrifice doesn't of course occur to either of them). Ollie, in his most ingratiating form, collects the orders, pointing majestically to each of the party in turn: 'Soda . . . soda . . . soda . . . and what will *you* have Stanley?' Stan smiles with pleasure: 'Soda'. With a courteous 'Pardon me' to the girls, Ollie turns on Stan—'Don't you understand? We've only got 15 cents. Now when I ask you to have a drink, you refuse. Do you understand?' (all this very deliberate). Stan nods, and Ollie begins on the same routine. 'Soda . . . soda . . . soda . . . and what will *you* have, Stanley?' 'Soda'.

'Just a moment, please. Pardon me, once more'. Then to Stan: 'Can't you *grasp* the situation? You've got to *refuse*'.

Stan's answer is magnificently typical: 'But you keep asking me'.

'But we're only putting it on. For the girls.' (This even slower, as if spelling things out to a backward pupil.) Understanding dawns.

Back to the routine. 'Now let's see. Soda . . . . soda . . . . soda. And my dear Stan what will *you* have?' Stan smiles proudly as he gets it right: 'I don't want anything'.

But it can't end so simply: one of the girls protests that he must have something. So Stan brightens up: 'All right, I'll have a banana split.'

As usual the climax of this gag (in the classic triple form) leads directly into new action. Ollie kicks Stan and is kicked back, then pushes him and is poked in the eye: he then explains smilingly to the girls 'Just playing together'. As he smiles he gives a final vicious pinch to Stan's arm.

The richest source of confusion for Stan is

Frame: Men of War, *with James Finlayson.*

language itself.

As early as *From Soup to Nuts* he is baffled by the instruction, given in a title, to 'serve the salad undressed', and dutifully returns to the table in his underwear—a scene which is nostalgically recreated a decade later in *A Chump at Oxford.* In between, sound has greatly increased the scope for this verbal literalism which doesn't replace, but complements, his already fertile 'visual' literalism. Much of the verbal detail recalls Lewis Carroll's *Alice* books, and its appropriateness to Stan's child-like persona is borne out, if one feels the need to check on something that's so instantly recognised as right, by Piaget's 'Language and Thought of the Child': see especially the chapter on 'Some Peculiarities of Verbal Understanding in the Child Between the Ages of Nine and Eleven', which is if anything a bit old for Stan.

Scram begins with Stan and Ollie up before a judge on a vagrancy charge. 'Do you plead guilty or not guilty?' Ollie: 'Not guilty'. 'On what grounds?' Stan: 'We weren't *on* the ground, we were sleeping on a park bench'.

Is there another comedian who could say this line without leaving the audience with some residue of resentment, however slight, against the script for a deliberate weak pun? Here, there is none: Stan is wholly and movingly in earnest.

It's a test line: anyone who winces at it in performance hasn't much prospect of ever liking Laurel and Hardy.

I say this not to sneer at such people: it's possible to find offensive or uninteresting a type of humour based on giving to an adult the thoughts and feelings of a child, and to refuse to take into consideration the things that can be done with it.

Harpo Marx in *Horse Feathers*, warned by Groucho that 'You can't burn the candle at both ends', gleefully whips out from around his person a candle lit at both ends. In *Them Thar Hills*, made two years later and perhaps glancing at it deliberately, Ollie's doctor gives him the same warning but is immediately put right by Stan who earnestly tells him 'We don't burn candles, we have electricity', and is launching into an explanation of the mains system when cut off by Ollie, who *can* understand proverbs. (A moment earlier, Stan has answered the doctor's warning against too much high living with 'Maybe we'd better move down to the basement'.) Harpo has an awareness of what he's doing which Stan generally lacks. Harpo, in the same film, produces a cup of hot coffee from his coat pocket. Stan's equivalent is to produce from his waistcoat pocket a salt-cellar to use on his hard-boiled eggs while visiting Ollie in the *County Hospital*. This is not invention but its reverse, the plodding conventionality of the family picnicking by the roadside with full kitchen equipment.

Nevertheless Stan has occasions of brilliance which are not incompatible with his literal-mindedness; indeed they represent its corollary. One can say that to grasp metaphor requires imagination; in another sense, it is more imaginative not to do so but to keep 'seeing' the literal reality which metaphor blurs. Indeed this is closer to the root meaning of the word. When Stan heard the expression 'On what grounds ?', he sees solid ground. He pictures things with intense vividness. When in *Going Bye-Bye* a convict threatens to catch up with them and twist their legs around their necks, he goes through the film giving a quick, tearful miming of this contortion at every hint of danger. And the reverse side of his 'simple' reading of the world is an inspired opportunism: when, in *Busy Bodies*, Ollie

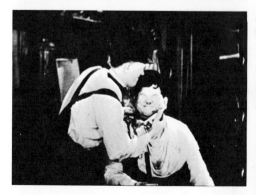

Frames: Busy Bodies *and (far right) the thumb-smoking in* Blockheads.

64

can't separate himself from the paintbrush which is glued to his chin, Stan removes the handle, soaps the 'beard', and shaves it off with a plane.

This complexity *within* Stan's simplicity shows the psychological insight that is behind his child characterisation, raising it at once above any charge of mere exploitation of idiocy.

The infant who hasn't yet mastered the reality principle is surrounded by a world which is still alive for him, a world with 'magic' potential. Given faith, why shouldn't the world of objects and cause-and-effect be willed into obeying the ego? Stan tries sympathetic magic in *Towed in a Hole*: shut away by Ollie to keep him from mischief, he draws a face on the wall, labels it 'Ollie', and pokes it in the eye. Usually he tries to will objects and natural laws into obeying him, in vain—only Stan could strain to pull himself up a wall by tugging on his own trousers (*Habeas Corpus*). In the feature films however he is several times rewarded with magical powers: striking a flame from his thumb, as from a match, in *Way out West*, putting tobacco in his fist and 'smoking' his thumb (real smoke) in *Blockheads*—it's a marvellous image too for the continuation of childhood (thumb-sucking)

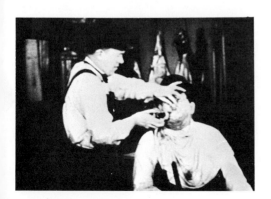

into adulthood (smoking—very important to Stan as a symbol of maturity in *Sons of the Desert*). In *Blockheads* again, Stan pulls down the *shadow* of a blind. He has games of near-magical dexterity in *Fra Diavolo* and *Babes in Toyland*, and is miraculously lucky with fruit machines, winning the jackpot first go in *Men of War* and again in *Way out West*. Also in *Way out West*—his most 'magical' film, though he's at the same time completely recognisable as the old, bungling Stan—he has to eat his hat after losing a bet. Despite initial crying, he enjoys it so much that

Ollie has to stop him from finishing it. When Ollie tries a surreptitious bite, he spits it out at once. He normally acts as Stan's foil like this, at first disdainful of his 'magic', then vainly emulous. In general, Ollie is about half-way to Stan's childishness. He understands proverbs, and can use sarcasm, neither of which Stan can, but he too can come to grief by taking others' sarcasm literally (as in *Pack up your Troubles*, in which they ask a fellow-soldier where to take the camp garbage and are told 'to the general's quarters'). He is capable, at times of tension, of doing a placatory tie-twiddle into the telephone (this perhaps only demonstrates that it's a nervous reflex as much as a means of communication), and it's he who gets relief from massaging Stan's foot, not the other way round, but on the whole he is too sophisticated (though this isn't the first word which normally comes to mind in describing him) to be Stan's equal either in literal-mindedness or in magic. In *Way out West* he does, finally, succeed in 'lighting' his thumb, but is so terrified that Stan has to come to his aid.

Frames: **Way out West** *and* (*right*) **Busy Bodies.**

OLLIE

If Ollie has some of Stan's childishness, he also slips naturally into the role of parent. This works in two main ways. It is he, rather than Stan, who supports or represents authority : he is the 'parent' trying to restrain or punish Stan or give him jobs to do. But when they attack authority together, he still has the parental role of spokesman and leader.

Neither can be summed up adequately in a chapter, but one can come nearer to doing justice to Stan by collation of details than to Ollie.

Stan was the creative half of the team in the studio, certainly, and a superb actor and mime, but Ollie is the richer, 'bigger' character.

A childish father-figure, he is a broader

version of Falstaff, a comparison that is to be made almost explicit in *A Chump at Oxford*.

Though it doesn't make much sense, really, to choose between Laurel and Hardy, most people will express an instant preference for one or the other, without having to hesitate and ask 'What exactly do you mean?'; there seem to be Laurel people and Hardy people the way there are Disraeli and Gladstone people. Try choosing ten 'great moments' from their films—rather a 'cult' exercise, it is true, but interesting in clarifying one's responses. Brilliantly clever though the best bits of Stan are. I would take most, possibly all, from Ollie; or if they are both involved (as in the laughing scene of *Scram*), it is Ollie at whom I would be looking.

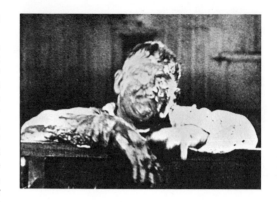

It is better perhaps to begin not with generalisation but with a specific area of his technique, the camera-look, which has the advantage of illustrating from the start his consummate skill as a film actor as well as filling in points about his characterisation.

To look collusively at the camera at all implies a certain kind of relationship with the audience that can't be taken for granted; when it is, as in the gimmicky aside-to-camera technique of *Tom Jones* and *Alfie*, the result can be to alienate us damagingly. Chaplin in his early films uses the camera-look delicately, usually to express mute appeal when thwarted, or apprehension, and so do other comedians including even Stan, but no-one has used the technique with such emphasis (frequent close-ups) or with such a range of expression as Ollie.

The camera-look exasperated. This is the basic one, the best-loved and the earliest to be perfected. It is to Ollie what the cry is to Stan. After suffering some pain or indignity like immersion in a pool (the end of *Putting Pants on Philip*), Ollie fumes in close-up. Or, it may simply follow some stupidity on Stan's part, and

vary from a resigned look flashed at us in medium-shot to a reaction of horror in which Ollie's mouth opens and his hands go up above his head. We get this in *Their First Mistake* when Stan brings out the feeding-bottle from next to his chest.

Quizzical. This is also common, and a big part of one of his staple routines: the long close-up which slowly takes in the nature of some disaster. For instance, when Stan's hot-water-bottle comes open at the start of *Leave 'em Laughing* and Ollie, adjacent in bed, begins to feel the moisture. Or in *Night Owls* when

Stan is helping him up over a wall and an ominous ripping sound is heard: Ollie 'freezes' and peers back over his shoulder and into the camera.

Apprehensive. Waiting, in *Way out West*, for Stan to winch him up to the balcony, Ollie catches our eye (medium-shot) and glances downward: we see that he has his fingers crossed. He can even use this special relationship to 'tease' his audience. In *Another Fine Mess* he is masquerading as the owner of a mansion and having to show round some prospective renters of it. The couple press him to play 'his' grand piano for them. He finally says yes, smiling ingratiatingly, but as he sits down to play, thus sinking out of frame, he darts at the camera a look of intense sick apprehension. Naturally we infer he can't play at all (and he doesn't in fact play the piano in any other film, often as he sings and dances)— but he does so with superb confidence.

Conspiratorial. We get this when Ollie decides to try eating Stan's hat when his back is turned, in *Way out West*, and when he licks the soupspoon in *One Good Turn* after showing his disgust at Stan's licking of it. Also, when he notices in *The Music Box* that Stan has a flex caught round his ankle and resolves to pull it. In *The Hoosegow* Ollie looks at us with indescribable conspiratorial glee as he reveals that he has a spare apple unknown to the warder. The warder sees him, and confiscates it. How easy it would have been to have the warder in turn give us a satisfied glance. But the convention is kept rigidly under control: no-one is ever on the same terms with the camera as Ollie.

Embarrassed. *Wrong Again* opens with Stan and Ollie working as stable-boys. Two men talking are suddenly struck by a forkful of

Frames: **Wrong Again** *and* (*left*) Towed in a Hole *and* The Finishing Touch.

manure coming from offscreen. Ollie appears and in a very extended close-up looks sheepishly at them, at us, and back at them.

In *Our Wife* he is dressing for his wedding when, thanks to Stan, he unknowingly loses his trousers. When he does look down and notice, he minces away with passionately coy looks and gestures at the camera—no-one else is present. One couldn't go further in treating the camera as a person, but it still doesn't come over as gratuitous. Interesting sidelights on Ollie's camera-awareness from within the films are in *Pardon Us*, where he insists that Stan smile sweetly for the prison photographer, and in *Sons of the Desert* where both of them are in a parade being filmed for a newsreel. Ollie drags Stan from the ranks and they hog the camera in close-up: a great scene which is also of relevance to the plot.

An earlier scene from *Sons of the Desert*, made in 1933, indicates what a subtle and varied weapon the camera-look has become. They are at a masonic convention where Charley Chase, as the life and soul of the party, introduces them to his repertoire of jolly games. He shows Ollie the flower in his lapel, saying 'I bet you don't grow flowers as good as this'. Ollie, in close-up, bends to smell it, and gets a

Frames: Liberty (*above*). *Still:* Swiss Miss (*right*).

jet of water in his face. He endures it, glances with horror at the camera (1), then is swallowed up in laughter and congratulations on being a good sport. He joins in the amusement but in the middle of a laugh darts another quick look at the camera (2) just to reassure us that he isn't taken in. Still in the same close-up, Stan reaches across to examine the flower and releases a new jet of water into Ollie's face. He endures it and gives a more fixed look of resignation (3). Chase is still going on about what a good time they're having: 'You boys must come over to my table'. Ollie, while he smilingly accepts, flashes us the most speaking camera-look of all (4).

Now we go out of close-up and into a medium-shot of them all at the table. While Chase orders champagne and settles them down, Ollie continues to show his misgivings (camera-looks 5 and 6). The breakdown of his misgivings—his unfortunate involvement in the Convention ethos and Chase's ideas of fun— is measured simply by his ceasing to look at the camera.

If Stan's feeling for Ollie is crystallised in the image in *Wrong Again* where he flutters back and forth between retrieving his own hat and trying to rescue Ollie from agonising pain, Ollie's action on top of the the skyscraper in *Liberty* (illustrated) can stand as an image of his feeling for Stan. Stan is hanging precariously from a girder. Ollie, crawling at great risk along it, struggles to pull him up. On the verge of success, he realises that he himself is beginning to slip underneath; so he hastily scrambles up and thus pushes Stan back to where he was before. All this is very quick and instinctive.

Both men are selfish; this 'realism' about Man and friendship is what makes the scenes so funny; but the two fundamental human motives which come into conflict in Ollie— the instinct for helping a neighbour, the instinct for self-preservation—go deeper than in Stan. His selfishness is of a much cheaper kind than Ollie's: fetching his hat or, in *Swiss Miss*, turning aside from Ollie, who is dangling over an Alpine gorge, in order to follow a St Bernard for a shot of brandy. What Stan is revealing, it could be maintained, is a greater

stupidity, but such stupidity is inseparable from selfishness just as in other films (e.g. *Sons of the Desert*) it is inseparable from innocence: he is too much of a child, in short, to be either unselfish or morally responsible. His promptings, in the scenes quoted, are those of a child clinging to a toy or bawling for food. He is softer than Ollie but also more callous: he can't conceive of altruism, and he only understands friendship as an extension of, or means to, elementary gratifications: food, warmth, cosiness. Perhaps the inchoate mass of his personality is a truer symbol of universal man, as containing in a purer state the childhood drives from which mature personality develops: Ollie in this case can stand for the same personality at a later stage of development when these drives have been worked into more abstract feelings: feelings for others, dignity, desire for achievement, etc.

Often he displays a premeditated viciousness of which Stan isn't capable. True, Stan will join in the slow rituals of retaliation, but he couldn't have *started* the rope-pulling in *Way out West*. The one really vicious action in *The Music Box* is Ollie's pulling of the flex to trip Stan—were the positions reversed Stan would no doubt have managed to pull it accidentally or from curiosity, but he couldn't have done it deliberately except as a direct response to provocation. Ollie coldly threatens in *Way out West* that he will string him up and leave him for the buzzards. Stan couldn't have said this. He responds predictably with a cry. But Ollie's coldness is only the obverse of his warmth. Stan may not use coldness as a weapon but he can reveal an indifference to friendship and to Ollie, underneath, which is more callous. The contrast is dealt with more systematically in the late features *Blockheads* and *A Chump at Oxford*, but it underlies all their shorts.

Early to Bed is an extraordinary *tour-de-force* made in 1928. One isn't surprised to find it generally written off between then and now as uninventive and uncharacteristic. They don't play their normal roles but are master and servant. The film has few gags and even these are mostly very direct, scarcely gags at all. Stan pushes over a delicately-balanced vase; Ollie, in pursuit, just manages to catch it, replaces it, and stands back to mop his brow in relief. Stan darts back, still in the same shot, to push it over again: it smashes. Much of the humour is still more simple, with Ollie standing by Stan's bed, pouring a jug of water gleefully over him, pretending to stop, then pouring again . . . .

The film consists entirely of their relationship. There are no other actors. (I think this is unique in their films, if one excludes *Brats*, where they double as their own children.)

Ollie inherits some money. Stan worries about what will happen to him; Ollie pleases him by taking him on as his butler. Their subsequent behaviour fits their status as master and servant (Ollie bullies Stan) and at the same time transcends it: informality breaks in. Stan tries to keep to his place as servant but he fulfils Ollie's wishes only when he drops this role and fights back: then, he becomes an equal and a friend.

At times, as the two men chase around the cluttered house, abandoning the normal master/servant rules, the film becomes an uncanny anticipation of the James Fox Dirk Bogarde relationship in *The Servant*. Both couples play a sort of hide-and-seek game; both knock over a vase on the stairs.

The film ends with Stan, having beaten up Ollie's house, pursuing him through it. Ollie takes refuge in a fountain adorned with gargoyle images of himself. He 'hides' by replacing one gargoyle with his own head, and spurting water like the others. Stan rests by the fountain and looks at the gargoyles, which have interested him all along. There now develops one of their finest 'open-ended' sequences, Stan watching curiously while Ollie tries to avoid discovery by keeping up an even spray of water. When he dries up, Stan, using the remedy he has found effective earlier for 'unsticking' the spray, bangs him on the head. When Stan turns away, Ollie dives down and takes in water. Stan remains there, weapon at the ready. It's another scene which is set to go on for ever. When Stan has got in five hard blows to Ollie's head, but isn't any nearer to understanding the situation, Ollie breaks the deadlock. Gradually his mask relaxes into a self-identifying smile. At the same deliberate pace he plays little games with the spray, laughs, splashes Stan, gets out, and sits down beside him. 'Let's forgive and forget and be pals again'. A two-shot, with Ollie's warm extrovert smile and Stan's shy hesitant one. Ollie ruffles Stan's hair. Stan does the same to Ollie who nods delightedly and gives him a playful push: he falls into the water. Still playfully, Ollie picks up the stick and knocks Stan on the head. Stan sits up in the water and looks resigned while Ollie laughs. The film ends.

So in a way the master/servant relation is re-established, but with the difference that it's informal and temporary: Stan will retaliate, and however angry it may make Ollie it's what he has recognised that he wants, deep down— they will be 'pals'. He has forgotten already the damage that Stan, the servant, has done to his house. This isn't the Tom and Jerry convention; it reveals Ollie's priorities, which misfortune may frequently deflect him from but not destroy. If his switch from tears to laughter at the end of *Big Business* is a definitive rejection of sentimentality, he does not reject sentiment. I find *Early to Bed's* last section very moving, like that of *A Chump at Oxford*

which 'answers' it twelve years later. To spell out its implications is alien to the tone of this very free film which depends so much upon momentary nuances of expression: its 'meaning' is concentrated in Ollie's beautiful slow smile from the fountain in which he (literally) affirms his humanity and appeals to Stan for the old friendship. But this in itself is a kind of parable, and the film a 'moral fable'. Friendship is more important than power and property. At the end, Ollie is stone and decides to 'become' human: how does he achieve this? By smiling. Psychologists have explained the origin of the smile, and thus of all humour, by reference back to the satiated set of the infant's mouth at his mother's breast. What is physically automatic grows into something conditioning our whole make-up. Whether this is sound or not, *Early to Bed* has offered a similar, imaginatively valid, kind of reconstruction. Smiling is for Ollie the most economical and natural way of relaxing his features to give the information that he is human, not stone. The equation is thus made: to be human is to smile. The smile can't avoid having all its usual connotations. Man is defined by his capacity for friendship and humour.

Such analysis may not make one understand the film any better, but what it may help one to understand is upon what the immediate 'recognition' and love are based which Laurel and Hardy get from such diverse audiences. To talk of warmth and humanity, even in connection with films which on the surface consist of two stupid men squabbling, will not necessarily be to retreat into sentimental abstraction. *Early to Bed* has simply given a more explicit account of the principles that inform all of their comedy.

It's always Ollie who leads, in any issue like this of friendship. In *The Perfect Day*, when they come to blows while preparing for

has been kind to them. His gestures of Southern courtesy are more than a form. He would not strike a lady as Stan does in *The Music Box* and *Sons of the Desert*, and he stops him from striking the nurse in *The Finishing Touch*.

To focus on Ollie's generosity is to bring out something important which is always there—but how does it relate to the violence which is the first thing anyone associates with Laurel and (especially) Hardy?

Frames: Leave 'em Laughing, The Music Box, and (*right*) Towed in a Hole.

the picnic, the wives are shocked: the two men look at each other in a lengthy two-shot, and Ollie, of course, is the one who breaks into a sheepish grin and reconciles them until the next mishap. Stan would have gone on looking blankly, stuck between his quarrel with Ollie and the wives' disapproval of it. One gets into the habit of *always* watching Ollie more closely in a two-shot. It's he who returns them from tears to laughter at the end of *Big Business*, and he who 'conducts' their laughter in *Scram* and in *Leave 'em Laughing*, as well as getting into it a much richer variety of facial expression.

It's Ollie who, when they both get roughed up separately at the end of *Below Zero*, runs around calling frantically, out of real concern, for Stan. He is jealous of their friendship in *Busy Bodies*: when Stan threatens to make friends with the fellow-worker who has humiliated Ollie, we feel his genuine hurt at a betrayal, unaffected by the anger he has been storing up against Stan in the previous scene. In *Scram*, it's Ollie who stops to help the drunk who has lost his car keys on a rainy night: 'What seems to be the trouble, neighbour?' In *One Good Turn*, it's Ollie who insists they must help the old widow who

Stan has no ideals; Ollie has. He has an ideal of friendship, of altruism, of tranquillity. Sometimes, he is on the point of attaining this. He shows a real aesthetic delight when things are going smoothly: singing as he dresses for his wedding in *Our Wife*, lovingly stacking the washing-up in *Thicker than Water* ('Now we're getting some place'), singing again as he prepares supper in the caravan in *Them Thar Hills*—there's an astonishingly long scene here during which everything goes without a hitch and we get a heart-rending vision of how things might be for Ollie: if only there were just one film where nothing went wrong for him . . . . These illusory moments of calm do more than create a dramatic irony for an audience who knows the complacency will be shattered: they deepen our understanding of Ollie's behaviour. His rage when frustrated is rage at the loss of his neat, ordered world, or of its internal correlative, his dignity; but the form which his rage takes itself expresses his ideal of order.

He reacts not blindly but coolly; at least, when he is goaded into retaliating hastily it's at once felt as a self-betrayal, and is followed by even greater loss of dignity.

His smallest gestures are neat and formal (ringing bells, signing his name) and where possible symmetrical (his manner of wiping mud from both eyes simultaneously, or of throwing away bricks which have landed on him).

Symmetry in retaliation: in the early silent, *Their Purple Moment*, Stan strikes Ollie's wife. Ollie is outraged, draws back his fist—and strikes Stan's wife. It is the one exception to his rule of courtesy to women.

Raymond Durgnat writes of their large-scale scenes of retaliation: 'How absurd yet how strangely persuasive are those "tit-for-tat" sequences, where Stan, Ollie and an antagonist or two, often James Finlayson, wait and irately allow the other to rip off his clothes, tear his jalopy to pieces or ruin his shop or his house. Each lets the other do his worst before retaliating, perhaps in obedience to some strange relic from the Code of the West, perhaps deliberately stoking up his own indignation and therefore strength, perhaps out of bravado, perhaps out of obedience to some streak of masochism which, if Laurel and Hardy films are any guide, must be more compulsive in human nature than commonsense would have us believe.'

I think there is something valid in all these associations, but that the key to them all is in Ollie's psychology and his ideal of order. After all, the Code of the West is itself something imposed in retrospect, to satisfy our longing for neatness and clarity, upon a reality which was 'realistically' messy. And it is reasonable to treat these scenes in terms of Ollie and not the others: even when he doesn't start the action himself, he is the focus of interest.

Ollie won't compromise: if things are not going to be perfect, let them be wrecked thoroughly. He may go to considerable lengths to avoid pain or disaster, but once caught he will not budge; by now it's too late for evasion, and to have a half-disaster only makes the readjustment of the balance, the restoration of equilibrium, more complex. Stan's instinct, in small matters, is to make do and mend. We see this in his tying together of the two ends of cable in *The Midnight Patrol*, and even in remarks such as this to Ollie in *Way out West*: 'Now you've got your clothes off, why don't you have a bath?'— Ollie, here and elsewhere, holds obsessively to the rule that you have a bath on Saturday night and only then. In *Busy Bodies*, where they work as carpenters, Stan 'planes off' a

strip of Ollie's trousers: true to his patching-up mentality, he sticks back the strip with glue on to Ollie's underpants. A bit later, cutting bristles from Ollie's chin, he snips off his tie (which detail no doubt has symbolic overtones. In *Oliver VIII*, his tie is cut off by Mae Busch). Naturally Stan restores it as best he can by hanging the pieces down from the top of Ollie's overalls. Very sadly and deliberately, Ollie picks it out from there and throws it away. Better no tie than a patched-up one; and better to put Stan *clearly* in the wrong.

When, in a lot of films, he receives a rain of bricks from above (usually down the chimney) he sits there stoically until he's quite sure the last one has come down.

Helpmates: when Stan carelessly throws a bowl of dishwater out of the window into his face, Ollie doesn't duck but stands there silently while Stan refills the bowl and again empties it in his face. The film is a succession of such accidents stoically endured by Ollie with scarcely any bid to redress them: he acts like a pedantic schoolmaster getting a perverse satisfaction from the number of blunders his

Frames: Busy Bodies and (right) unjamming sink in Helpmates *and waiting for bricks in* Dirty Work.

pupil makes, as if by just recording and even provoking these he were being more loyal to his own vision of perfection than by admitting that a goal of something lower than perfection were any more worth striving for than utter disaster.

The Perfect Day. They are trying to get the car started. Ollie goes to crank it, telling Stan, who's anxious to help, 'You can throw the clutch out. That's *easy*'. Stan reaches down ominously to the floorboards and starts pulling: while he does so, Ollie watches with mounting horror but what he will not do is to

intervene or to warn: Stan duly extracts the clutch and throws in into the road. Ollie can thus fume, slowly fetch it, and gird himself up for apt retaliation. This is the 'tit-for-tat' procedure on a more intimate scale.

In *Angora Love*, and again in the remake *Laughing Gravy*, Ollie goes one logical step further. He fetches a jug of boiling water to pour into a tin bath. At the last minute Stan, without malice, moves the bath. Ollie, unmovable, continues to pour the water smugly on to the floor. It's Stan who is in the wrong.

Angora Love provides a nice link with the large-scale tit-for-tat scenes. After more clumsiness, Ollie is soaked. He picks up the bath and throws the contents at Stan, who ducks: the water goes over their landlord, Edgar Kennedy. Searching for appropriate ammuntion, Kennedy takes the jug and goes to the next room to fill it from the tap. A visitor (Charley Hall) gets involved, and all four of them successively come out to the tap. The filling of the jug serves as a metaphor for 'filling the tank' of their resentment. Better a full, satisfying flood than a series of little splashes of irritation. The rhythm of this scene, and of films like *Big Business*, is the rhythm of a cistern, violent 'flushes' interspersed with pauses while the cistern steadily fills. Pauses for contemplation prevent the protagonists' anger from going off at half-cock and wasting itself. Their coolness allows them to act with the decisiveness which in real life we attain only in agonised reconstruction of events: 'Now when he did that, what I *should* have done was....' Stan and Ollie and their antagonists don't have these worries, which helps to explain why they are able to dismiss their grievances so quickly from memory. They are purged, and we who watch are purged with them.

Frames: Chickens Come Home.

EARLY FEATURES

For the last two chapters, I have been drawing material from the films of different periods, covering a span of twelve years, and I leave a full chronological account to the Filmography at the end, which includes plot-summaries plus comments on points of interest not mentioned already.

The main development in their career is the gradual switch from shorts to features. The overlap period lasts from 1931 to 1935.

It will be seen from the Filmography that after 1930 they make fewer shorts from year to year and that the quality becomes on the whole less consistent. There are fewer crowd scenes, and sometimes a sense of skimping in sets and resources. This can be attributed in part to the contraction of the shorts market, with more investment thus going into the longer films, but there must have been other factors, too, in the change of emphasis. Roach's own desire to be more 'respectable' and get away from what he saw as custard-pie slapstick; the greater scope offered by sound for comedy on a more intimate scale; the simple desire to do something different and not let the mass-fight ending become a predictable formula. In any case, they had never depended on having crowds and elaborate resources. *Early to Bed*, their simplest film and one of their best, was made in 1928. Any generalisation is difficult.

If the later shorts contain few masterpieces, there are still excellent films in the old style like *Them Thar Hills* (1934). If they seem to be relying increasingly on gimmicks, with the dream framework of *Oliver VIII* (1934) and their dual roles in *Twice Two* (1933), these are only repeats of devices used previously in the rather *less* interesting shorts of 1930: *The L & H Murder Case* and *Brats*.

The fact is that their only time of unbroken inspiration was 1928-29, on either side of the introduction of sound, working under McCarey's supervision. Understandably, they did not keep this level up, though 1932 is almost a return to it with only one weak short out of six (*The Chimp*) and the other five all, in their varying ways, admirable (*Any Old Port*, *The Music Box*, *County Hospital*, *Scram* and *Their First Mistake*). But generalisation about good and bad periods, even, would be misleading: from 1930, strong and weak tend to alternate unpredictably. Nor is it useful to favour the films credited to a particular director: James Parrott made *The Music Box*, Raymond McCarey *Scram*, James Horne *Laughing Gravy*, George Marshall *Their First Mistake*, Charles Rogers *Them Thar Hills*, and Lloyd French *Busy Bodies*, but all of them worked on less impressive films as well. The man in effective control was Stan.

But it is clear enough that their talent in 1935 is undiminished. Ollie's face may not have quite the boyish openness of their first films, but his command of expression is still wonderful and the timing of both as sharp as ever. What makes their weak films (ominously) weak is a plot which gets in the way—not allowing them either to initiate action themselves in the classic way, or to create little 'free-wheeling' scenes for themselves in the plot's margin. The problem of finding the right kind of plot, solved so effortlessly in the early years, became increasingly acute as the films grew longer and more subject to advance planning.

The true Laurel and Hardy feature films are listed below. They also made guest appearances in other films, and did a series of films after 1940 for M.G.M. and Fox; these are included in the Filmography.

All the films listed here were produced for the Hal Roach studios except for *Flying Deuces*, and on this, too, they had something like the old degree of freedom which was soon to be denied them.

1931	*Pardon Us*	episodes
1932	*Pack up your Troubles*	episodes
1933	*Fra Diavolo*	comic opera
	Sons of the Desert	organic whole
1934	*Babes in Toyland*	comic opera
1935	*Bonnie Scotland*	episodes
1936	*The Bohemian Girl*	comic opera
	Our Relations	Stan production
1937	*Way out West*	Stan production
1938	*Swiss Miss*	comic opera
	Blockheads	retrospective
1939	*Flying Deuces*	old style
1940	*A Chump at Oxford*	retrospective
	Saps at Sea	old style

This shorthand labelling is not very adequate, but provides a rough idea of how their career developed.

Their 'episodic' films do not call for very detailed treatment. They are less satisfying than the shorts of the same period. In fact, *Pardon Us* began life as a two-reeler but was expanded for economic reasons when its prison sets proved too expensive to build.

They go to prison for selling liquor, escape, but are recaptured. They inadvertently foil a mass-escape plot, and are released as a reward for their heroism.

Some of the scenes inside the prison are good, and in the main line of their work, particularly the one in which the warden dissuades them from joining in a hunger-strike by a graphic description of the turkey dinner they will be

80

missing. Moreover, this furthers the plot: it's because they go to the meal (consisting of gruel) that Stan is on hand to foul up the escape plans. All too many of the scenes however lead nowhere and seem to be there just as uninspired padding: in the prison classroom for instance, or at the prison dentist's—a remake of the middle part of *Leave 'em Laughing*. There is a long dull slab in the middle of the film in which, after escaping, they take refuge on a cotton plantation with their faces blacked: it includes the only uninteresting song and dance act in their films (a Spiritual from Ollie, and a dance from Stan). Stan himself aptly summed it all up as 'a three-storey building on a one-story base'.

The best parts of *Pack up your Troubles* are better than anything in *Pardon Us*, but it is still more loosely episodic, lacking the degree of unity given by the prison setting.

Stan and Ollie join up to fight in World War I. They progress from the training-camp to the front, where a comrade of theirs is killed; when they get home they visit his baby girl, find she is being ill-treated by foster-parents, and remove her. They now have to track down the grandparents—but the name is Smith. On this thread is hung a series of adventures, some of them neat. They see a poster for a boxing match, Steamboat Smith v Kid McCarey (private joke: Raymond McCarey co-directed the film). They find Steamboat's training camp, and Ollie tells him cheerfully 'We've got your son's child'. His response is 'Blackmail, eh?' and a right to the chin which knocks Ollie cold. Cut to the next episode. There's also a real anthology piece, the only part of the film now remembered, in which the child, preparing for bed, decides she will tell *Stan* a bedtime story, and sends him easily off to sleep. The end, too, is interesting. They finally

Still: Pack up your Troubles.

hand over the child to her grandfather, a rich banker. He is overjoyed and insists that they stay to dinner, pending some proper reward; when he says casually to the butler 'Oh Meadows, three more to dinner', we think what an enviable well-ordered life this is, in which this sort of instruction can be murmured at a few moments' notice, and what a cloyingly happy ending for Stan and Ollie. But these feelings are neatly exploited. The cook emerges from the kitchen in a rage, finding this order the last straw. And we recognise him as the soldier who (early in the film) was the cook to their company, and whom they unwittingly got into trouble—he sees them, draws his kitchen knife, and goes after revenge. With their exit, the film ends. Family sentiment stays behind. This is in fact similar to the final touch in *Pardon Us*. The Governor, giving them their discharge, thanks them for their public-spirited co-operation and

dwells on the potential good that is in them; as he modulates into pompous words their eyes glaze over. He ends with a hope they will be able to start again in life where they left off. This is something Stan can understand: he brightens up and asks if they can take his order for some liquor. So the film ends as he irately chases them from his office. As at the end of *Big Business*, so in these films, by being cut off abruptly from a scene of sentimental cosiness, they are able to keep their integrity. It is an idea that will recur.

Pack up your Troubles starts with an army episode of half an hour which scarcely connects with the rest of the film. *Bonnie Scotland*, a film which goes conveniently with these two although they have made three other films in the meantime, puts its army episode second. Again its connection is tenuous. They have come to Scotland (a not very Scottish-looking Scotland) for the reading

of the MacLaurel family will. Stan gets a pair of bagpipes, but no money. After some desultory adventures, they go along to a tailor's shop where suits are being offered on approval. They sign their names for this but find that they've come to the wrong place and have signed on for a Highland regiment going to India. Such continuity as there is comes from the further coincidence that some of the characters we have seen already are posted to this same camp. But these people have little connection with Stan and Ollie anyway— there is a very definite plot and sub-plot. The main romantic plot is so stilted as to be, presumably, someone's attempt at pastiche. A more interesting intrigue is the backstairs one between Lady Vi's maid, Millie, and the company sergeant: the suggestion of an affair between James Finlayson and Daphne Pollard, two faithful supporting characters, gives an entirely new dimension to the film. The only

Stills: Pack up your Troubles, Bonnie Scotland.

thing to do now is to mention Stan and Ollie's good scenes. There has been some entertaining business in the first half, of the sort they could do in their sleep, but go on presenting freshly: playing with hats, etc. The second part has the classic scene where, on a route march, Stan finds himself out of step, but succeeds in communicating *his* step to the rest of the platoon—and finally to the sergeant alongside (Finlayson). Also two very characteristic scenes with just the pair of them, when they have been sentenced to extra duty. While they sit waiting, Stan puts a finger in his mouth and blows hard: the front of his army helmet lifts up. Ollie is intrigued and tries to do it. But we can see that Stan is simply pressing the back of the helmet against the wall behind him as he blows. Ollie doesn't see this, and keeps trying. As he doubles himself up with

83

the effort, Stan reaches over and tips the helmet up with his finger. Ollie gets excited, and keeps trying to do it again. Sgt Finlayson gapes. This kind of scene, of which the prototype is in *Fra Diavolo*, is already becoming a pleasant convention. The prototype of the next scene is in *The Music Box*. They are set to spear up leaves from the parade ground and put them in a bin. Bagpipes are heard; and their work gradually dissolves into a marvellous impromptu Scottish dance, an interlude which in itself would make the whole picture worthwhile. Perhaps the plot defects make one underestimate, in retrospect, the many real pleasures to be got from a film like this. If I am grudging about these episodic features, it is through comparing them not only with the better shorts, but with the 1933 feature film *Sons of the Desert* (released in England as *Fraternally Yours*).

SONS OF THE DESERT

Sons of the Desert, the fourth of their full-length films, is, I think, the most perfect of them; it doesn't, like its possible rivals *Blockheads* and *A Chump at Oxford*, depend on a knowledge of their career as a whole to get its full effect. (Some critics, in fact, give the preference to *Way out West*.) It is also the best of their 'domestic' films. Each of them is married, and we see a lot of the wives.

The Sons of the Desert are a Masonic type of fraternity to which Stan and Ollie belong (Ollie in real life was a master mason). They are both committed to attending the annual convention, i.e. annual binge, but have yet to inform their wives. From his deportment at the meeting which opens the film (at the reading of the line from their constitution that 'the weak must be helped by the strong', he gives a wonderfully condescending look at Stan), and from what he says on the taxi-ride home, we gather that Ollie will simply inform his wife while Stan meekly asks for permission. The film is a gradual and subtle modification of our expectations; and the interest is sustained by the fact that the way they are treated is related to what they deserve. It is an exploration of the different degrees of 'innocence' of Laurel and Hardy.

The two families live next door to each other. When they get home only Mrs Hardy is there; she treats Stan with the scorn he invites, but isn't altogether polite to Ollie either. When the convention issue comes up, she is very firm indeed. Ollie devises an elaborate plan to feign illness, and have a fake doctor prescribe a cruise to Honolulu where he knows she couldn't accompany him since she hates sea travel—Stan can therefore be deputed to go with him, and they can slip off to Chicago and the convention instead.

This is Ollie's elaborate, calculating form of deceit. Stan goes along with it; but his natural level is more what we have seen already, namely the surreptitious biting of the apples which Mrs Hardy displays in her living-room. These apples, though he doesn't realise it, are wax. It's a most beautiful symbol of Stan's innocence: he eats the apple (knowledge of good and evil) but it's only a 'dummy' knowledge, and he stays innocent. Moreover, in this symbolism the literal level of 'what's happening' reinforces—expresses—what it stands for symbolically: Stan's complex mastication of the wax apples conveys a personality determined but slightly lost, 'choking on' experience. Stan's life is a *continual* effort to eat the apple and lose his innocence in the world—this is the third apple Mrs Hardy complains she has missed this week—but he never makes it. Stan may think he is deceitful but he isn't, and he keeps betraying himself. Ollie, however, is. The film is a development of the moment in *Come Clean* (1931) where Stan and Ollie are trying to prevent the woman whom they have saved from drowning from following them home and thus causing trouble with the wives. (Mae Busch, who plays the vamp in *Come Clean*, is Mrs Hardy in *Sons of the Desert*.) She asks them where they live. Instantly, side by side in the shot, Ollie points in the wrong direction, Stan in the

Still: Bonnie Scotland. In India with Sgt. Finlayson.

85

right one.

Feigning illness, and submitting to the fake doctor's attentions, Ollie revels in his deceit, darting conspiratorial looks at the camera. Stan abets him—but with a depth of incomprehension which is shortly revealed. The scheme works, Honolulu is recommended, Mrs Hardy won't go, perhaps Stan will go instead? But Stan says no: he can't do so because he'll be at the convention in Chicago. . .

However, Ollie takes charge, and gets them to Honolulu, i.e., to the convention, where they have a good time. The Honolulu cruise ship sinks and the wives rush frantically to the ship's office for news; unaware of this, Stan and Ollie come home bearing pineapples. Stan picks up a newspaper, and soon turns from the front page to the inside in order to read the 'News from the Clubs'. Ollie glimpses the headline about the disaster, and at once sees all its implications. He shows it in horror to Stan who, when he succeeds in taking in its relevance at all, merely remarks what a good thing it is they *didn't* go to Honolulu. His dumbness is inseparable from a deep moral innocence.

These distinctions crystallise in the final part of the film which is, together with the end of *A Chump at Oxford*, the high point of their work in features. The wives have already been made suspicious by a strange 'phone-call from Chicago and wonder if the boys could possibly have done any lying to them; Mrs Laurel announces 'Why, Stanley wouldn't dare lie to me. I hate to think what would happen if he ever did.' In the middle of their worries about the sinking, they learn the truth via a newsreel film of the convention which shows Stan and Ollie disporting themselves prominently and gloriously. Now, they agree to test their husbands against each other by seeing if either of them can be induced voluntarily to tell the truth. Meanwhile Stan

86

and Ollie are camping out, planning to arrive home simultaneously with the rescue boats, but a storm forces them back early (it's Stan who insists on going home, though Ollie has at first been ready to stick it out).

So a perfect test situation is set up, with Stan and Ollie unaware that their wives know everything. It's like the testing by the Duke at the end of *Measure for Measure*.

In the presentation of the wives, there has been a fascinating balance between comic and serious. In some scenes they are apparently just conventional bullies, in others their sense of insecurity is very touching.

Stan has by now grasped what the issues are. Between them, they fumble together a story. Ollie is the first to be asked point blank, by his wife, if the story is true. Looking all injured innocence, he says it is. Then Mrs Laurel asks Stan. There is a long, blank close-up of him listening to her elaboration of the question. He screws up his face and cries and starts pouring out his confession. Cut to a *static* camera look of exasperation from Ollie, which has twice the usual hardness since it contrasts so strongly with his familiar turn of the eyes to the camera within the shot.

Mrs Laurel follows the tearful Stan out of the door (they have been in the Hardy half of the building), carrying her rifle. We're encouraged to wait for violence: rifles wielded at the end of Laurel and Hardy films have never yet been left unfired (*Wrong Again, We Faw Down, Blotto, Laughing Gravy, The Midnight Patrol*), and we know already that Mrs Laurel is an expert shot.

Ollie, alone with his wife, puts on his most innocent, pouting baby-face. He plays wonderful 'displacement activity' games on the table with his fingers. When his wife keeps advancing, he tries to disarm her with playful twiddles of his hat, and baby-noises. The scene would fascinate an anthropologist. His wife sweeps past him to the kitchen, and begins to pile up crockery.

Back to Stan—who is on a couch, drinking, eating chocolates, cosseted by his wife, looking rather dazed; with no fuller an understanding of this situation than he had of his and Ollie's plotting. Crashes begin to shake the houses' dividing wall. Stan strolls next door to visit Ollie, and compares notes. Justice has been done.

The film is very much more than a moral schema. It is deeply funny, with a great richness of detail, meticulously acted and plotted, and directed with an understanding of the timing which Laurel and Hardy's personalities dictate (direction is credited to William A. Seiter, who made no other film with them). They have mastered the longer form: the film has as tight a unity as any of the shorts, but uses its extra length to good purpose. The

Masonic pastiche, and the whole scene at the Convention (about 20 minutes of film), is admirably sharp, never losing touch, as do sections of other features, with the main thread. The song-and-dance cabaret number *Honolulu Baby*, for instance, quite elaborately staged, is not just an interlude but closely integrated: it is functional in reminding them of Honolulu (thus starting a new plot-development), and it forms the basis of two later scenes in which Stan and Ollie very enjoyably recreate it. Ollie's brother-in-law, a quintessential fraternity bore, is played by Charley Chase, an excellent Roach comedian in his own right and the brother of their long-time director, James Parrott.

Still: from the end of Sons of the Desert *(released in Britain as* Fraternally Yours*), with Mae Busch as Mrs Hardy.*

COMIC OPERAS

Before *Sons of the Desert*, Laurel and Hardy had already made *Fra Diavolo*, from Auber's comic opera, and there are three more films in this convention in the next five years: *Babes in Toyland*, *The Bohemian Girl*, and *Swiss Miss*.

Fra Diavolo is the best of the series. Stan and Ollie (or Stanlio and Ollio) are good citizens of 18th-century Italy who are retiring complacently with their nest-egg when they are surprised by bandits. Penniless, they decide to turn bandits themselves—i.e., they change from one familiar role to the other, from bourgeois to outcasts. They hold up a peasant, who tells them such a convincing tale of misery that they end up weeping and giving money to *him*; they then hold up the great bandit chief himself, Fra Diavolo. So they have the character common to both their roles, that of bunglers.

The parts are natural ones, then, for Stan and Ollie, adapted and expanded for them without doing too much violence to the original or to the tradition of the comic sub-plot. Nor is there anything wrong in consigning them to a sub-plot: it is one solution to their problem of how to graduate from their natural length, the two-reeler, to full-length stories. (*Sons of the Desert* is another.) The 'plot' can keep on providing situations for them to improvise freely on; at the natural time their bit can end and the plot move on. Even when plot and main characters are uninteresting as in *Babes in Toyland*, they provide situations for Stan and Ollie with rather less strain than when they have to keep labouring to move the plot along themselves. There is a difference between the 'imposed' arbitrary plot of which they are the centre,

88

and the conventional comic opera plot which operates in a sphere above them. And the relation, or lack of relation, between them and the main story may itself be meaningful.

Charles Rogers directed the Laurel and Hardy scenes; Hal Roach, in his only official work as director, did the others, which are better than some have given him credit for. The main plot has Fra Diavolo posing as a Marquis and trying to rob a noblewoman, who is travelling with her husband, of the jewels and money she carries about her person. Since Lord and Lady Rocburg are played by James Finlayson and Thelma Todd (who was Mrs Plumtree in *Another Fine Mess*), the scenes with them are not at all out of key with the rest. Finlayson as a cuckolded aristocrat is good casting. The other remnant of plot from the original concerns a servant girl and an officer and is less interesting, but we are never away from Stan and Ollie for long enough to be impatient. The way they become involved in all this is to be taken on as servants by Fra Diavolo. When he captured them, he had sentenced Ollie to hang, with Stan as his executioner. This provides a good scene in itself, but a reprieve comes when Stan bungles the job and Fra Diavolo finds that he needs them anyway as accomplices whose faces will be unfamiliar. He takes them with him to the hotel where the Rocburgs are staying, and proceeds to woo her ladyship.

Stan as a servant has difficulty with his cocked hat. They both exchange deliciously coy glances with a pair of servant girls. They play games: kneesie-earsie-nosie and finger-wiggle. Kneesie-earsie-nosie is the first of

Stan's formal games of dexterity. He slaps his knees, then simultaneously pulls his nose with the left hand and the left ear with the right hand, then slaps his knees and reverses the pulls. He continues the sequence briskly. Ollie, at first scornful, tries it and fails. A running gag through the picture has the landlord, through sleepless nights, trying as well. Stan's face says that nothing could be simpler.

Stan has a superb drunk scene, leading into one of uncontrollable laughter recalling *Scram* and *Leave 'em Laughing*. He drinks a drugged glass of wine meant for Lord Rocburg, and is thus incapacitated when they have to do their dirty work for Fra Diavolo. They have opportunities for double-takes, for hitting each other, and for Stan's cry. In fact, they have very full scope; and their comic villainy neatly parallels the benevolent banditry of Fra Diavolo, who finances the young lovers' wedding at the end.

Fra Diavolo has always been popular and their next two operatic films, *Babes in Toyland* and *The Bohemian Girl*, deservedly rather less

Still: with Dennis King in Fra Diavolo.

89

so. *Babes in Toyland* was remade by Disney in 1962 without any apparent emphasis on the Laurel and Hardy parts; they are less integrated than in *Fra Diavolo*. Again the direction is divided, Charles Rogers sharing it this time with Gus Meins. Stan and Ollie, in the Rogers part, play Stannie Dum and Ollie Dee in a sickly Toyland where the romance between Bo-Peep and Tom-Tom is threatened by the miser Silas Barnaby, and where the punishment for crime is to be sent down a well into Bogeyland. Their job is in the toyshop. Strangely, with all its nursery-rhyme characters, the film is not altogether suitable for children. The ending, where the bogeymen, hairy, ape-like monsters, escape up the well and invade Toyland, only to be repulsed at the last moment by Stan's army of life-size toy soldiers, is like *King Kong* only more frightening. One shot in particular, of the bogeymen snatching screaming children from their beds, is enough to give a child nightmares (which is confirmed by friends who saw it as children).

Like *The Bohemian Girl* and *Swiss Miss*, the film stands or falls by the quality of Stan and Ollie's isolated turns. Even Finlayson is not here to support them. One neat three-part gag is worth recording. They have been caught in an attempted burglary of Silas's house, and sentenced by 'Old King Cole' to a public ducking. Ollie is ducked first. Then:

(1) News comes that Silas, now that Bo-Peep has agreed to marry him, withdraws the charge. The sentence is cancelled: Stan is free. Naturally he doesn't realise that he is one-up on Ollie as a result, but Ollie does realise.

(2) First 'reversal': Ollie pushes Stan into the pond to get even.

(3) Second reversal: Stan, struggling out, holds up the watch which Ollie had entrusted to him for safety and which has now got soaked.

Stan has another manual dexterity game, with missiles and a stick. When Ollie wants to try it, and insists he can do anything Stan can, Stan shakes his head and does a rapid mime of kneesie-earsie-nosie, which strikes home. This is a very rare reference back to another film: the only equivalent that comes to mind is *Tit for Tat*, which looks back to incidents in *Them Thar Hills* in which the same four characters were involved. Even this reminder of *Fra Diavolo* doesn't stop Ollie from trying—and failing.

Stan's other big scene is yet another one in drag. To foil Silas's plan to marry Bo-Peep, Ollie makes Stan dress in white and veil his face. Only after the ceremony does Silas unveil his 'bride' for a kiss. The twist in this is that Stan *is* now married to Silas, and Ollie won't hear of his being let off. Stan cries, because 'I don't love him'. (It's typical of the loose plot that nothing more is heard of this— unless we're meant to assume that the final 'and they lived happy ever afterward' includes Silas-and-Stan.)

Ollie has rather less scope. On the whole it is the pattern of the mid-'thirties that Stan regains pride of place. His ingenious or magical side is given freer rein, while the films grow more remote from the everyday respectable world that provides the most telling context for Ollie.

His best scene here is in the raid on Silas's house. The plan is for Stan to deliver as a 'present' a big box with Ollie inside it, and for Ollie to get out in the night and steal the mortgage which is Silas's weapon against the nice people. All goes well until Stan, delivering it, says not only 'Good-night Silas', but 'Good-night Ollie', and Ollie answers back. The scene ends, after his discovery, on a beautiful protracted close-up of him looking out of the box, with his most sheepish expression, playing very deliberate games with his fingers along the box's edge. (These recall the finger

games at the end of *Sons of the Desert*.) It is increasingly the case with these films that they are valued for the concentration which Stan and Ollie can get into tiny moments like this.

For instance: at the end of *The Bohemian Girl* they are both tortured. Stan is screwed down while Ollie is stretched. (It is one of the series of tiresome 'freak' endings: they emerge, for the last shot, as dwarf and spindly giant. Other freak endings come in *Liberty*, *Dirty Work*, *Flying Deuces* and—more interesting —*Thicker than Water*.) While Stan is being screwed down, we see only his eyes looking out

Still: Stan about to be tortured in The Bohemian Girl.

of the chamber. After each turn of the screw he opens them further, and these immobile isolated eyes are fantastically expressive.

Swiss Miss opens with their visit to a cheese-shop, trying to sell mousetraps. They fall, and cheeses cascade down from the shelves on to Ollie's head. One recalls innumerable scenes where he has received a rain of bricks from a damaged chimney; he makes this falling-cheese scene into a summary of all of them. Three cheeses fall, then a pause: Ollie slowly looks up with a movement which expresses at once hope that fate will withhold any more pain, and certainty that it will not. At precisely the critical moment a fourth cheese falls, hard. Ollie receives it with stoical immobility, screwing his face up in disgust. Over the years, he has made this ordinary slapstick gag into a routine that can express a whole attitude to experience, a life-style. Though their cinema, like television today, ate up material at a great rate, thus contrasting with the famous old music-hall system of taking the same act round and polishing it lovingly for years, nevertheless Stan and Ollie contrived something similar by their endless re-use and re-polishing of bits of business within new situations. In these mid-'thirties films they have an ideal field for this sort of work, a relative vacuum, where they are neither much helped by, nor responsible for, the plot.

The Bohemian Girl has some excellent bits, usually on the lines of Stan against Ollie. There is also a timely appearance by Finlayson, near the end. Stan has a solo set-piece which is one of the things most often and affection-ately recalled by their loyal, now middle-aged fans of the 'thirties (another is the kneesie-earsie-nosie game). It is like the drunk scene of *Fra Diavolo*, except that there Hardy was with him, handing him the wine which he didn't have a place for, apart from his own mouth. Now he is on his own with a barrel of wine, some bottles, and some piping. As the start of *Swiss Miss* gives the essence of Ollie and objects-from-the-sky, so this scene is the essence of Stan overwhelmed by objects. The pipe leading from barrel to bottles takes on a life of its own which Stan can't cope with. When he has filled one bottle and is looking for another, the pipe keeps spurting wine, so for convenience he puts it in his mouth. Objects

accelerate away out of his control: the longer he takes to find the next empty bottle, the longer the pipe stays in his mouth, and the longer he therefore takes to find the next bottle. It's a measure of Stan's greatness as an actor that one takes for granted, by now, his incredible expertise in 'pacing' a scene like this, all done in one long take. (It is marred slightly by the inept continuity of the cutaway shots showing the contents of the barrel going down.)

The story, and the songs, are the weakest so far. Stan and Ollie in a band of gypsies—a girl wandering from a nobleman's house, lost, is adopted by Ollie—she grows up with them—their travels bring them back in the same route years later—she's found and restored to her home. The ending resembles that of *Pack up your Troubles* in that Stan and Ollie, having restored the long-lost child to its family, are released into the bleak air. In *The Bohemian Girl* this is particularly callous since they have been tortured on the premises, while the girl who grew up with them sits smugly in her ancestral home, incurious about their fate—a kind of reversal of the character of Eppie in George Eliot's *Silas Marner*. Some of the early scenes have deliberately pushed the sentiment of the Silas/Eppie kind of story over into sentimentality, with for instance long-held shots of Ollie beaming at the girl while she sings. The exaggeration of this, and its reversal at the end, amount to a rejection of the whole sweet pseudo-pastoral convention. The sentimentality is like the weeping in *Big Business*, and the treatment of Stan and Ollie at the end has something in common with the final chase towards the horizon. While this (as before) preserves the integrity of Laurel and Hardy, it can't quite make up for the protracted sickly passages of the story.

Swiss Miss does not appear to derive from a comic opera original, but the singing done by the leads, and the tinselly Swiss backgrounds, bring it into the same category as the other three.

The film gets them to Switzerland as mousetrap salesmen who choose the best potential market, and involves them in the 'plot' by a device already familiar from shorts (*Their Purple Moment, Below Zero*). The cheese shop owner has paid for their services, and they celebrate with a big meal at the local hotel, bullying the staff in the course of it. When they offer payment, it turns out to be fake money; the manager, after hearty laughter at their joke, sees the truth and sets them to work

Frames: (opposite page) Stan filling wine-bottles in The Bohemian Girl, *and (above) the serenading in* Swiss Miss.

in the hotel kitchens. In this hotel are staying the two romantic leads, both dull. The girl 'uses' Ollie to make her lover, a singer, jealous. (Again, this is an idea used elsewhere, in *The Fixer-Uppers*.) The only useful function of the plot is to provide a series of situations in which Stan and Ollie can work freely. There are some beautifully polished routines during their atoning work in the kitchens, but *Swiss*

93

Miss is remembered above all for two distinct episodes. One is Stan's contrivance to get brandy from a suspicious St Bernard by plucking a chicken and throwing the feathers in the air to descend as 'snow'. (Like the wine scene in *The Bohemian Girl*, this is excerpted in full in the *Crazy World of L and H* compilation.) As usual, this is consummately played, though it is not one of my own favourite scenes, being more of a gagman's idea carried out by Stan than an irresistible expression of his personality. The other big scene is that made famous by James Agee in his essay on *Silent Comedy*:

'Laurel and Hardy are trying to move a piano across a narrow suspension bridge. The bridge is strung over a sickening chasm, between a couple of Alps. Midway they meet a gorilla.' The scene marks the climax of their love-hate relationship with pianos, prominent in a number of their films and never left undamaged.

Wrong Again: They put a racehorse on top of a grand piano, which collapses.

Big Business: Stan, in the attack on Finlayson's house, brings out the piano and hacks it to bits. When he sees the policeman standing

over him, he starts trying to put it together again.

Night Owls: In the house of the police chief which they are burgling, they accidentally set off the pianola music. While the chief, roused, asks his butler 'Who's playing the piano at this time of night?', they stuff a bearskin rug inside to try to deaden the noise.

Another Fine Mess: Ollie plays the piano, the lid of which crashes down on Col. Plumtree's fingers.

In close-up, the keys hammer on Stan and Ollie's faces. When they begin to emerge, Finn slams the lid down, which sends them both through the bottom of it on to the floor.

In *Swiss Miss* the piano ends by crashing down into the gorge, as does the gorilla. The gorilla survives and later re-appears on crutches to chase Stan and Ollie away in yet another freak ending.

Frames: (opposite page) Swiss Miss; *(this page)* Wrong Again *and* The Music Box. *Still: (below)* Swiss Miss.

Beau Chumps: Ollie bounces high into the air and lands on the piano, wrecking it.

The Music Box of course *is* the piano (or the crate containing it?)

Way out West: Fleeing from Mickey Finn (Finlayson), they hide inside his grand piano. Finn doesn't see them, and is going out of the room when he hears strange chords. Ollie has indignantly forced Stan to move over. Finn sits down at the piano, and with a Hardy-like glance at the camera plays energetically.

LAUREL PRODUCTIONS

Stan was clearly not satisfied with the unevenness of their longer films, and between *The Bohemian Girl* and *Swiss Miss* he took charge of two far more tightly integrated stories: *Our Relations* and *Way out West*. They are the only two which give him official credit for 'A Stan Laurel Production'.

Our Relations is the antithesis of the loosely constructed opera films. It is so intricately plotted as to be rather a strain: there isn't room left for them to develop their best leisurely routines.

Half the film is a kind of *Son of Sons of the Desert*, with Stan and Ollie as respectable fraternity members, older and settled, finding the main excitement of their existence in the repetition of idiotic Masonic ritual. However, they have twin brothers Alf (Laurel) and Bert (Hardy), disreputable sailors whom they believe to be dead. These arrive in town, and the predictable confusions take place.

It is the only film, except for *Twice Two* and *Brats*, where they play double roles, but, since they appear together only in the final scene, the technical complications are not so great. They simply play alternately the two familiar

Publicity photograph from Our Relations, *with Arthur Housman (the perennial drunk in Laurel and Hardy films).*

versions of their characters, the bourgeois and the outsider, bringing the two into confrontation. In theory this is magnificent, and one should be able to interpret the film like this:— Stan and Ollie are complacent, conventionally married American citizens, who have damped down all their anarchic energies or sublimated them into Masonic rituals. Alf and Bert represent the past which they are determined to forget. When at the start they are confronted with an old photo of all four of them together, dug up and sent them by Hardy's dear old mother, they daren't show it to the wives since they would be appalled to learn that the whole family wasn't respectable. Keeping this secret from their wives makes the entire plot possible (since they have to believe that the Alf and Bert whom they meet are their own husbands), but it is also justified thematically. As he burns the photo Ollie says, 'We'll burn our *past* behind us'.

Alf and Bert represent the 'truer', irresponsible side of Laurel and Hardy; they not only represent it but bring it to the surface in Stan and Ollie themselves by creating difficult situations for them. It is the respectable Stan and Ollie who, blamed by their wives for what Alf and Bert have done, suddenly burst out in defiance and resolve to have a night on the town. They have always wanted this; their wives, as they show, have always expected it. It is Stan and Ollie who, under provocation, enter into the last of the true 'tit-for-tat' sequences with James Finlayson. The irruption of Alf and Bert is therapeutic, clearing repressions.

Alf and Bert for their part are striving for respectability, trying to save money and 'get some place'. The end, where both pairs meet and recognise each other, stands for their re-integration. Stan and Ollie's 'past', their energy, is recognised and absorbed back into the present.

I offer this analysis half-seriously while stressing that an effort of abstraction is needed: the themes aren't fully realised in the film as they are in comparable 'analyses' of Laurel and Hardy, *Blockheads* and *A Chump at Oxford*. There are some pleasant scenes, particularly with the wives (Mrs Hardy is played again by Daphne Pollard), but the two 'halves' of Laurel and Hardy aren't sharply enough distinguished: too much of their time is taken up with the mechanics of mistaken-identity farce. It's significant that I haven't had reason to cite a single incident from the film in other connections (contrast *Way out West*, which is so fertile in imaginative details). Most noticeable is the fact that there is little sense of the old relationship *between* the Laurel and the Hardy of either half: they don't cause each other trouble. Consequently, the violent potential even of Alf and Bert isn't much felt, and the 'dialectic' between the two sides of Laurel and Hardy is more academic than a summary suggests.

Our Relations still works well as a neat and entertaining comedy, and is perhaps the most respectable of their films, with antecedents going back to Plautus and Shakespeare (*The Comedy of Errors*); Borde and Perrin, in their *Premier Plan* booklet on Laurel and Hardy, bracket it with *Blockheads* as their masterpiece, but I would argue that to appreciate Laurel and Hardy fully is to prefer to it not only *Blockheads* but even a scrappy film like *Babes in Toyland*.

Way out West however succeeds in reconciling the old richness of detail with the greater strictness of form evidently desired by Stan. It is full of brilliant scenes, many of which I've described already in different contexts, and these are held together by a firm story-line and a consistent 'Western' atmosphere. It is their last film with James Horne, and James Parrott, another old collaborator,

worked on the script.

Stan and Ollie come to Brushwood Gulch to hand over a deed to a gold-mine. The orphan girl, Mary Roberts, who inherits the mine, is working in the town saloon for her guardians, Mickey· Finn and his wife the 'Serio-Comic Entertainer' Lola Marcel. The first ten minutes show us life in the saloon; they are so good, in contrast to the normal framework for Laurel and Hardy, that one almost regrets the switch to Stan and Ollie en route, especially since their first scene is overlaid by bad, unfamiliar music. But their part livens up with Stan's parody of *It Happened One Night*: he hitches a lift for them on a stagecoach by showing an expanse of leg, and inducing the driver to stop with a squeal of brakes.

Finn, by passing off Lola as Mary, gets the deed from them. Lola induces Mary to sign a receipt for it, pretending that it's a paper ensuring that all they do for her as her guardians will be legal. This simple shot, with Lola's 'smiling villainy' and Mary's quiet trust, provides not only a plot but a 'world' for Laurel and Hardy, who are duped like Mary but who finally help her innocence to win. This shot evokes Griffith, as does that of the cringing girl forced to marry the heavy in *Any Old Port*. One recalls, too, the children snatched by bogeymen in *Babes in Toyland*. Certain scenes with Stan and Ollie themselves in a crowd of hostile soldiers or criminals (most strikingly in *Pardon Us*) create a sense of helplessness which the comic tone can't altogether blunt.

The film starts during their journey to Brushwood and ends with their departure: it is

Still: (left) Way out West. *Ollie's hat has had chunks bitten out by Stan. Frames: (right) fighting for the will in* Way out West, *with James Finlayson and Sharon Lynne.*

continuous in time, apart from one ellipse between day and evening: it centres on their loss and then recapture of the deed. There is just enough plot to give the film unity without getting in the way. This permits not only some great scenes in the main line of the story (the attempts to evade Finn; Stan's reduction to helpless laughter as Lola struggles to get the deed from its hiding-place under his vest; their efforts to rope themselves up the outside wall of the house) but also diversions, easily absorbed. These include 'surreal' jokes —Stan's hat-eating and finger-lighting—and three glorious musical sequences. A dance when they arrive, the duet 'Trial of the Lonesome Pine', a final song with Mary. It is the most musical of their pictures, and the last in which they sing, apart from *Flying Deuces* (unless they do so in one of the post-1940 films, not all of which I have seen). Considering how good are Ollie's singing and both men's dancing, their restraint is remarkable, for they could easily have made a musical number into as much of a trademark as Stan's cry. When they do sing and dance, it's never felt *just* as a gratuitous interlude, not even in *Flying Deuces* where they take time off from a chase to the death in order to accompany the camp band in 'The Good Old Summer-Time'. It is part of the temperament of both that they can be distracted, like children, from business, however serious, by what is immediately appealing. Even in *Way out West* they join in the first two numbers rather than starting them.

Way out West is picked out by both Basil Wright and David Robinson as the most successful feature. While I prefer others as being finally more meaningful, it is certainly the one in which they pack end to end the greatest number of pure gags, while avoiding any sense of strain.

Frames: Way out West, *chase continued.*

LAST FILMS

They seem to age rather suddenly, Ollie in particular. In *Blockheads* he is much heavier, and fatter in the face, which means that his range of expression is diminished and, most important, that he can no longer command his 'innocent child' look. Stan's face is now more visibly lined. This ageing makes it increasingly hard for them to do their old form of comedy 'straight'. Both *Blockheads* and *A Chump at Oxford* are consciously analytic and backward-looking, getting to a certain distance to say something about them and their relationship. I shall postpone comment on these two films and deal first with the loose ends of their career.

Flying Deuces (which follows *Blockheads*, in 1939) is an expanded remake of *Beau Chumps*. Charles Middleton again plays the Foreign Legion commandant with whom they don't get on, and their reason for joining is again Ollie's disappointment in love. But the picture is adapted to this later stage in their careers. They are American tourists in Paris, a more middle-aged occupation than usual. When Ollie decides to commit suicide for love, he takes it for granted Stan will come with him: 'Do you realise that after I'm gone there'd be no one to protect you?': this self-consciousness about their relationship belongs to the later films. The most striking development is that they are further separated than before from normality. Their humour and individualism are more extreme and they shrink back less easily into conformity. In *Beau Chumps* they

struggled to keep in military formation but got detached from the rest; here, in their first parade, they reduce the whole company, in the best of all their army scenes, to a balletic shambles. They do not just subtly infringe military rules: when they recognise on parade an officer whom they met in Paris, they overflow with bonhomie despite his outrage, calling out 'Don't he look swell' and, even as they are marched to the guardroom, 'Hey, where are you going to have dinner?'. They do not, as in *Beau Chumps*, naively request their release, to be soon cowed by a refusal—they are massively indignant, walk into the commandant's office asking 'What's the big idea,

Frames: song and dance in Way out West. *Still:* (*right*) Flying Deuces.

103

keeping us waiting like this?', and leave on his desk a note which he describes as the rudest he's ever read. The delicate balance between conformist and anarchist in them is broken. They flee from pursuit, but pause to sing with the camp band; in prison, Stan plays a Harpo-like solo on the bedsprings. Finally they escape in a plane (hence the title).

This broadening out of their comedy, giving them a touch of the Marx Brothers, is at times exhilarating and is understandable at this stage of their careers, but is clearly dangerous also since once their unique 'everyman' quality is

104

Stills: (above) Beau Chumps, *with Charles Middleton, who also plays the commandant in* Flying Deuces; *and (right)* Saps at Sea, *with Ben Turpin.*

lost it is only a short step to a coarser kind of farce.

In *Saps at Sea* (two films later, following *A Chump at Oxford*), they are scarcely in a recognisable real world at all. The 'surreal' gags no longer relate so closely to Stan's own consciousness. In their apartment, they find the plumbing all switched round: turn one tap and water comes out of the other, etc. The

woman next door has a fridge that plays music and a frozen-up radio. They contact the plumber—who turns out to be Ben Turpin with no less of a squint than before. (Contrast the 'realistic' use of the squint in Turpin's previous appearance in their work, as the magistrate in *Our Wife*, where he married Ollie not to his fiancée but to Stan.) The scene where Dr Finlayson examines the sick Hardy is full of 'impossible' jokes. The second half of the film, where they are adrift at sea (hence the title) with an escaped convict on board, has its climax in a meal which they are forced to prepare for him. They have no food, so they produce a fake meal with string for spaghetti, bits of sponge for meatball, bits of belt for bacon, tobacco juice for coffee; all of which they are then forced to consume themselves. Again this is taking further a device used more 'realistically' in earlier films, but it seems to derive more from Chaplin and *The Gold Rush*. Their comedy has been absolutely distinctive because rooted so firmly in the characters; take their devices a small step further and they become unexceptional echoes of other people's work, of a kind difficult, anyway, to bring off

as late as the 1940s. *Saps at Sea* is enjoyable, but it is getting away from the real Laurel and Hardy into a more nebulous 'gag' cinema, the kind of comedy which it was their distinction a dozen years earlier to transform from within.

After *Saps at Sea* they worked not for Roach but for the big studios, Fox (six films) and M.G.M. (two), both of whom were, they found, unwilling to let them work out their films in the conditions they were used to. They took the scripts they were given and did them the studio way. So they had no chance to experiment with other possible ways of coming to terms with advancing years.

These seem to have been years of great frustration and unhappiness, particularly for Stan as the creative half of the team.

No·one has had much to say in favour of the post-1940 films, least of all Stan and Ollie themselves. Most of them have gone quickly out of circulation and been forgotten. Judging

Stills: (*left*) Saps at Sea, *with Richard Cramer as the convict and Harry Bernard as the policeman; and* (*below*) Dancing Masters, *with Robert Mitchum.*

from those I have seen, and from synopses, they are stories which could have been written for anybody, padded out with re-creations of old L & H routines which lack either a meaningful context, or the old timing and range of expression, to give them life. *Dancing Masters* (1943) opens with Laurel and Hardy in comic costume, as dance instructors. They have often dressed up before—Ollie's naval uniform at the end of *Helpmates*, their Oriental dress in *Our Relations*, Stan's frequent drag— but never in their own films were they reduced to doing so without careful grounding, gratuitously. Their job as dancing masters has no relevance to what follows. Their technique has lost its beautiful *necessity*. The plot limps on through another depressing, arbitrary dressing-up scene (Stan as a foreign professor), and reminiscences of various shorts, including a flat remake of the entire auction episode from their last one, *Thicker than Water*. One doesn't get the impression of a complete lack of sympathy in the direction (which, as in several of these films, is by Malcolm St Clair, a veteran director of some reputedly interesting twenties comedies), but of a more radical limpness infecting the whole project.

They stopped making films in 1945; had a plan in 1947 to film in England, which came to nothing; then made a comeback in France with *Atoll K* (1951), known here as *Robinson Crusoeland*. After this, they did some music-hall touring, and were at one time set to make a series of comedies for Television; however, Ollie had a stroke before they could begin.

Stan in turn had been very ill during the shooting of *Atoll K*. His dreadful appearance makes the film almost unbearable to look at. When he is knocked over, one wonders if he can ever get up. By some freak, his illness makes him look more like Boris Karloff than the old Stan, and Ollie's voice and appearance are both much coarsened. (Happily, Stan was

soon to recover, and looks quite healthy in photographs taken near the end of his life.) They are like two old end-of-pier comedians doing a Laurel and Hardy imitation, not very well—right down to the ritual ending, their final scene in any film:

H: Well, here's another nice mess you've gotten me into!

L: Well, I couldn't help it (cries)

dialogue which has small relation to the actual situation they've been left in. At one point in the film, Stan proposes a toast and raises his glass so high that he deposits it on a rafter in their ship's cabin. He 'drinks', and gulps realistically. When he fetches the glass down, it's empty. This is in line with the style developed in the last of the good features, but the gags are no more integrated than the dialogue exchanges into any total framework (symptomatic of this is the separate credit to Monty Collins for 'Gags'). The plot has Laurel and Hardy with friends on a Pacific atoll setting up a tax-free Utopia. All great comedians imply a vision of society, but the dim explicitness of these scenes makes a sad end to the series of anarchic visions started by *The Battle of the Century*.

Still: Atoll K.

BLOCKHEADS

Blockheads and *A Chump at Oxford* are companion pieces. The former postulates a change in Ollie, the latter a change in Stan, thus transforming their relationship. In each, the new relationship is seen to be wrong and the old is restored.

Blockheads has a prologue set in the trenches of 1918. A platoon including Ollie goes over the top, leaving Stan behind, in spite of his 'Gee, I wish I was going with you', to guard the trench. A flashy montage sequence brings us up to 1938; Stan is still there and he has not altered. His routine is an image of the conventional, 'literal' part of his nature. He

Still: Blockheads.

about-turns in the hole which twenty years of turning have worn away, knocks off at the regulation time, and serves himself lunch: as he throws away the can a panning shot follows it to show us the pile that is the debris from twenty years of beans. Stan's acting, when he suddenly gets the news that the war ended in 1918, is, on a serious level, superb. (This quite long scene is mysteriously absent from the British television version, which does, however, have material that is not in the 16 mm print. But TV is emphatically not the ideal medium for Laurel and Hardy films.) We now cut to Ollie, back home and oblivious of his existence.

Ollie without Stan turns out to be almost irredeemably horrible. He's been married only a year, but his domesticity is more cloying than in any of his earlier 'married' films. When his wife, who's sulking because he's forgotten their anniversary, asks him what happened a year ago, his first effort is 'Was that the day I fell off the bicycle and grazed ma' knee?', and one really feels this to have been an index of his life's eventfulness, and his mind's smallness, when he has to go on to beg for something extra on his 75 cents daily allowance in order to go out and buy an anniversary present. This domesticity, his fatness, the self-parody of 'Pardon me for one hour' which he says to Mrs Hardy as he leaves (compare his catch-phrase 'Pardon me for one moment'), the fact that his first real gag is a crude exploitation of his weight, which Hardy in fact always hated (a midget gets out of the lift and he gets in; the lift crashes headlong to the ground floor)— all this creates a feeling of seediness in which it's hard to separate character from actor. Even his grimace to the camera, as he claims not to have forgotten the anniversary, hasn't been much consolation, for it implies not 'Damn my wife', like its earlier equivalents, but 'Oh dear, I've offended her'; it comes from within a George Gambol-like acceptance of his

situation. This then is Ollie without Stan, deep in a rut; his first scenes have been vivid enough to guide our responses as we watch him recover his full humanity. Redemption is at hand even now. As he goes out, the porter shows him a paper with a featured story of the Forgotten War Hero, with picture (Stan, garlanded). He looks, and returns it: 'Well, how in the world could anyone be so stupid? I can't imagine anyone being *that* dumb.' Then a double-take: 'Oh yes I can'.

Stan meanwhile is at the Soldiers' Home, relaxing in the grounds. He sits on a bench to read the paper, but finds it uncomfortable and decides to move to a wheelchair that is standing empty nearby. The only drawback is that there is a board in the way which stops him from extending his right leg. After some experimenting he gets off, tucks his leg under him, and sits. This is the kind of scene, alone with slightly recalcitrant objects, in which one could watch Stan for hours. Ollie has now arrived to seek him out. He walks along jauntily, beaming at the prospect of a sentimental reunion. As he catches sight of Stan, Stan happens to scratch his right knee—a rather horrible shot, in spite of what we know and Ollie doesn't. There follows a fine close-up of Ollie, his smile turning to sadness at the sight of his friend's disability, then back to a determined, make-the-best-of-it smile: he advances.

Stan returns his greeting casually and goes back to his paper, but then it sinks in. He makes to get up but Ollie hastily stops him. Their reunion is pleasant, even though it pales before what is to come. Stan: 'Gee, I'm glad to see you.' 'I'm glad to see *you*.' 'Have you missed me?' 'I certainly have.'

Ollie shows a fine generosity in insisting Stan must come home with him, although we

Still: Blockheads.

● ●

wonder already what his wife will think. He
describes the great meal she will cook them:
steak, mushrooms, seven-layer chocolate cake...
Stan's only query is 'Any beans?'.   The two
sides of Stan: he can eat rubber (*Their First
Mistake*) or felt (*Way out West*) with relish,
but his ideal is the same dish of beans for ever.
Ollie, who might once have been scornful, is
indulgent: 'You can have them if you want to'.
He impresses on Stan: 'I want you to remember,

from now on my home is your home'. As he
wheels an unprotesting Stan over to his car,
they are an image of a pair of old comrades in
their twilight days, all passion spent. Stan
talks to him: 'You know, Ollie, this is just
like old times, you and me being together . . .
You remember how dumb I used to be? Well,
I'm better now.'

Stan wants a drink of water, so they stop
by a faucet. Stan is going to get up but Ollie

naturally won't hear of it: he hands Stan the nozzle and turns the tap. Of course Stan manages to direct the jet on to Ollie, completely soaking him. We see memories stirring, but restraint wins. He comes back to the chair, pats Stan affectionately on the back, and pushes ahead—no recriminations, not even a look at the camera.

Another veteran now comes up and claims the chair back for his friend, who owns it:

Ollie now has to carry Stan. So immediately, Stan's legs are palpable. From now on they are Laurel and Hardy once more, for the obtuseness works both ways: not only is Stan showing no curiosity about his free ride, but Ollie is feeling and seeing, yet not seeing, two

Frames: Blockheads (*left and below*). *Ollie encourages Stan to try out the automatic garage-door-opening mechanism. Before and after.*

feet. Even when he puts down Stan in retrieving his hat, and is then helped up by him, he goes on as before, humping him to the car. Recognition doesn't come until after they have got into and fallen out of it. Then at last, back comes the true Laurel and Hardy dialogue and, after twenty years, some old Hardy looks.

H: Why didn't you tell me you had two legs?
L: Well, you never asked me.
H: Get in the car!

Stan goes round to the passenger door, muttering to himself 'Well I always *had* two legs.'

'You're better now!' Ollie puts the quotation marks round this, very audibly.

To confirm that he has not changed, Stan goes on to create an archetypal disaster. Ollie sends him forward to shift the truck parked in front, so they can get the car out. Stan contrives to tip a full load of sand back on to it. The scene is nicely directed: we don't see the result until after Stan has driven forward, stopped, and noticed the displacement of load; at the same time Stan does, we see Ollie's head, with hat still firmly on, protruding from a hill of sand. His emotion is so powerful, incapable as it is of release in action, that it finds a completely new expression: an incredulous, high-pitched exhalation of breath. The scene fades out as Stan scoops off the first handful of sand.

So Stan is still dumb and Ollie's indulgence towards him is unnatural. This is the point the film has clearly been leading to, and the second half, as we anticipate, shows the familiar destructive Laurel and Hardy in action. But it isn't so mechanical as this sounds. Though Stan is dumb, he is also inspired: two of his best 'will-power' tricks come in *Blockheads*, the shadow-blind and the thumb-smoking. As for Ollie: when for the first time in twenty years he feels the impact of Stan's bungling, he rages at him, but his anger doesn't endure.

We cut from the burial of his car to their return, in the same car, to his garage, and he is quite happy to let Stan try out the automatic door-opening mechanism. Nor does the destruction that results deter him from taking Stan upstairs to his home, and insisting on his right to do so against the uncharitable opposition of his wife. 'How often have I told you not to bring your tramp friends round here?' 'But Toots—Stan is different.' He could hardly treat Stan with more warmth if he *did* have an amputated leg, or if he had neither 'pretended' to have one nor submerged and then wrecked the car; the more damage he suffers, the more loyal he is to their friendship. Much in the second half of *Blockheads* is rather gentle, old-style Laurel and Hardy, and might on its own seem disappointing—and this is not a film which, by itself, is likely to convert anyone unsympathetic to them—but it has something in common with the serene late style of directors like Ford and Renoir: coming as it does after the developments of the first section, which restore their self-knowledge, it acts as a relaxed affirmation of all that they and their work stand for against the Mrs Hardy values by which Ollie had been seduced —the idea of a friendship based on frankness and conflict. For if, in the words once again of Raymond Durgnat, Laurel and Hardy keep throwing up images that are 'visionary crystallisations of the human condition', the whole body of their work, transcending all the comments one may make on parts of it, constitutes such a crystallisation: the dizzying spiral of endlessly renewed disaster, rage, reconciliation represents, on a level of comic expressionism, a realistic, dynamic vision of honest human relations.

The increased emphasis on Ollie's warmth and loyalty, shining through discouragement, is carried over into the climax of *A Chump at Oxford*.

A CHUMP AT OXFORD

● ●

A Chump at Oxford (made shortly after *A Yank at Oxford*) was evidently expanded during production by the writing-in of new scenes. It is curious, and perhaps relevant to this, that the credit titles at the end cover only the second half of the film, ignoring even James Finlayson in his penultimate Laurel and Hardy role. But *A Chump at Oxford* is more of a unity than the other padded-out films because it has a framework strong enough to absorb, at least in retrospect, the early material. The film is a re-enactment of their whole career together. The early scenes represent their work in shorts, and contain some direct

Still: A Chump at Oxford.

Still: Stan as Agnes in Another Fine Mess, *a role he repeats in* A Chump at Oxford.

echoes. They are looking for jobs, waiting at table, sweeping the roads. At the employment exchange, when a call goes out for a maid-and-butler team, Ollie accepts the job and makes Stan dress up as the maid—a maid with the same name, Agnes, and the same glorious flaxen wig as in *Another Fine Mess*. Their job is to wait at a private dinner-party; the hostess, again, is Anita Garvin, and the host James Finlayson (a repeat of his part in *The*

Second Hundred Years). Stan again serves the salad 'undressed', though there is the extra factor that he is drunk, having misinterpreted Finlayson's instructions to 'take all those cocktails'. Chaos comes more rapidly than before. Finlayson chases them out with a rifle, and the episode ends with a quotation from

Wrong Again: a constable (played by the same actor, Harry Bernard) charges in furiously with his pants shot off.

Next, they are street-cleaners. When they break for lunch, Ollie's meditations echo *Towed in a Hole:* 'Well, here we are at last. Right down in the dust. I wonder what's the matter with us. We're just as good as other people, yet we don't seem to advance ourselves. We never *get* any place.' They resolve to go to night-school, but their lives are changed quicker than they expect. The bank on whose steps they are lunching is held up. The robber, escaping, slips on their banana skin, and is captured.

The bank manager wants to reward them. They explain they are uneducated. 'Diamonds

Still: A Chump at Oxford, *with Wilfred Lucas as the Dean.*

in the rough, eh? And all you want is a little polish, the proper setting.' He sends them off, for the best education money can buy, to Oxford.

The banana skin, which has not infrequently landed them in trouble, makes them prosperous. Can one also, remembering their early work with Roach, read a private meaning into the fact, presumably calculated, that the bank which they both save and are financed by is prominently entitled the Finlayson National Bank?

The bank manager's words about 'the proper setting' call to mind the middle period of Laurel and Hardy's career, in which their comedy was enveloped in more elaborate plots and production values. The Oxford part of the film provides a context of considerable feebleness, so feeble as to be good, because it evokes so well the worst aspects of their 'vehicle' films. From their arrival at a two-dimensional Oxford they are pounced upon by a dreary crowd of students (among them Charley Hall and Peter Cushing) who play practical jokes, chant student songs, and talk about 'the pater'. They misdirect Stan and Ollie into an unlikely-looking college maze, and later into the Dean's quarters on the pretext that these are their allotted lodgings. The scene in the maze serves as a metaphor for their mid-career: rather lost, all they can do is to forget their surroundings and be themselves. In some ways their scene on the bench, where a ghostly 'third hand' keeps insinuating itself from the hedge behind them, is the summit of their comedy. In a stagey set and a contrived context, with the camera holding them in prolonged two-shot, they just do the scene, an isolated 'turn', and make of it a memorable sketch of the working of Stan's mind. The timing of both is uncanny. Eventually, the ghost emerges and frightens them both off.

The next scene shows them taking full possession of the Dean's house, and leads up to his return and his confrontation with a superbly indignant Ollie. Stan's dumbness is increasingly stressed. Looking at the decanter they have emptied, he tells Ollie 'There's no more nightcap'. 'Well, what would you do in a case like that?' A pause of several seconds while Stan thinks hard, then looks up brightly: 'Go and get some'. He has never before been quite so coldly presented as a moron. All this is a preparation for the last section of the film. After clearing up their misunderstanding with the Dean, Stan and Ollie are shown to their proper rooms where they meet their scout, Meredith. Astonishingly, he at once addresses Stan as 'Your Lordship', and tries to persuade him that he is Lord Paddington, a student who years ago lost his memory and wandered off. 'The greatest athlete and greatest scholar this university ever boasted of—and oh, what a brilliant mind!'

Ollie is amused and contemptuous. 'I've known him for years and he's the dumbest guy I've ever known—aren't you?' 'I certainly am.'

But Lord Paddington lost his memory when the window of this room slammed on his head, and Stan now leans out of the same window, preparing to escape a crowd of students who are coming to attack them. When the window falls once more, Stan is Lord Paddington. (As with the banana skin earlier, a stock 'pain' device now does something useful.)

Stan's Lord Paddington is amazing: one really does have to keep reminding oneself that it's not another actor. He massacres the students, and also throws out Ollie, who returns protesting. Ollie hasn't time to be baffled by Stan's sudden strength, he is too hurt by the affront. 'Stan, don't you know me?' Stan turns to Meredith: 'Who is this coarse person with the foreign accent?'. When Ollie reminds him of their days spent sweeping the streets together, he is ejected again for impertinence.

After a time-lapse we find Lord Paddington re-established as athletic and intellectual king of Oxford. Ollie is his servant, and they address each other as 'Fatty' and 'Your Lordship'. The Dean calls in to ask Stan if he can spare time to talk with a visitor from Princeton, Professor Einstein, who is 'a bit confused about his theory'. Ollie's camera looks are frequent and eloquent, but he has been stunned into subservience. In his absence Stan tells the Dean: 'Pardon my valet being so horribly stupid'. 'Why do you tolerate him?' 'Oh, he's got a jolly old face, you know—breaks the monotony—and besides, he helps to fill up the room . . .'

When the Dean goes, Stan, in a scene more painful than any of their slapstick, has a go at Ollie for his general slovenliness. He makes him stand up straight, pull his chin in ('both of them!'), and walk around under his direction. Ollie trips and falls. When Stan deplores this clumsiness, it is the last straw. He tells Stan

Still: A Chump at Oxford.

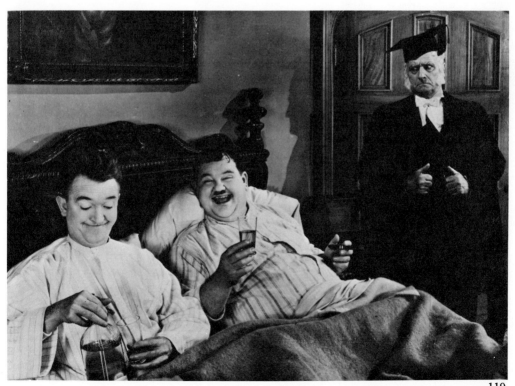

what he thinks of him, packs his bags, and is on his way out of the door and to America when he hears Stan, the old Stan, asking where he's going. The window has slammed on him a third time. After a brief talk at cross-purposes, Stan starts crying helplessly, and it dawns on Ollie that, miraculously, they are equals again. 'Stan!'—in a brief two-shot he hugs him with joy, looks down for a moment at the double-chin which was jeered at, forgets it, and smiles. On their renewed, joyful embrace the film ends.

In itself this final ten-minute section is marvellous, with Ollie creating a humiliated figure reminiscent of Emil Jannings in *The Last Laugh* or *The Blue Angel*. It becomes interesting in a further way if one looks at it in the loosely biographical terms I have been applying to the rest of the film, and earlier to certain shorts like *Putting Pants on Philip*. It's difficult to know anything of Laurel and Hardy and avoid at once seeing it in this way. Stan Laurel, in reality, was closer to Lord Paddington than to 'Stan'; he was British, and he was the brains behind their films, working on them at every stage while Ollie just acted. Leo McCarey testifies, what John McCabe doesn't go into, that he insisted throughout his career on being paid twice Ollie's salary. When he sits behind a desk telling his valet 'That's better . . . now walk around   . . . let me see you', he could be a director casting or rehearsing. Ollie's camera looks, even as they protest against this subservience, are on another level a testimony to it. McCabe quotes this recollection by Charles Rogers.
At times Stan would deliberately hold off shooting 'camera looks' until the end of the shooting day at a point when Babe would be dying to get out on the [golf] course. The result is that some of those exasperated looks that you see Babe give are *really* exasperated looks!

This isn't to suggest that Stan behaved to Ollie like Lord Paddington, off-camera—they apparently got on well together, always—but the scene remains a most powerful dramatisation of the gulf between Stan's screen self and real self. The return at the end of the film to his dumb persona oddly anticipates what happens to his career in that, with the partial exception of *Saps at Sea* immediately afterwards, he is henceforth confined to his role as Stan: he's not able to come behind the camera and, as it were, be Lord Paddington. The ending has *some* of the overtones of Prospero throwing away his book and staff.

John McCabe, and David Robinson before him, quoted another Shakespeare passage (*Twelfth Night*, Act I scene iii) to suggest the clowns' tradition to which Stan Laurel belongs.
Sir Andrew Aguecheek: Sir Toby Belch! How now, Sir Toby Belch!
Sir Toby Belch: Sweet Sir Andrew!
Sir Andrew (to Maria): Bless you, fair shrew.
Maria: And you too, sir.
Sir Toby: Accost, Sir Andrew, accost!
Sir Andrew: What's that?
Sir Toby: My niece's chambermaid.
Sir Andrew: Good Mistress Accost, I desire better acquaintance.
Maria: My name is Mary, sir.
Sir Andrew: Good Mistress Mary Accost . . .
Sir Toby: You mistake, knight.

Alec Guinness and, more recently, David Warner, have played Aguecheek in a recognisably Stan Laurel way. McCabe calls this exchange 'a verbal gag of the kind Laurel and Hardy would use if Christopher Fry instead of H. M. "Beanie" Walker had written their dialogue'. He might have pointed to *Beau Chumps*, in which this occurs:— Stan makes a

Still: Stan as Lord Paddington, Ollie as his valet, in A Chump at Oxford.

foolish remark to which Ollie, who is lovesick, replies 'This is no time for levity'. While Stan looks puzzled, Ollie launches into an ecstatic description of his fiancée. After a pause, he asks Stan 'Haven't you got anything to say?'. He has: 'What does levity mean?'. Ollie fumes, but is interrupted by a knock at the door. Stan at once picks up the phone and says hello, explaining that 'There's someone knocking on the phone'. Ollie, still fuming, tells him 'That's levity'. Stan says 'Hello Mr Levity' down the phone but gets no answer and so goes to the door. He takes a telegram from the delivery boy: 'Thank you, Mr Levity'. Because Ollie is so keen to read the telegram he doesn't put Stan right, and the joke can, characteristically, be renewed. When Stan, in the numbering-off scene already described, gives his Hollywood phone number, the camp commandant warns him 'This is no place for levity', and we see, even in medium shot, something stirring in Stan's brain: he's on the point of some new disastrous remark when forestalled by Ollie.

The point is, then, that Stan doesn't need any playwright to give him dialogue that is better than Aguecheek's. This example is nothing special. We should not underestimate them. Ollie too could play in *Twelfth Night*. He could play Sir Toby Belch, in a double act with Stan, and certainly one of the attitudes he embodies is given in Sir Toby's 'Dost thou think, because thou art virtuous, there shall be no more cakes and ale?'. But Sir Toby is too intelligent, and too limited. There are scenes of Malvolio's in which Ollie would be magnificent: though he might not have realised his cold, 'virtuous' side, could anyone have done better the scene beginning 'Sweet lady, ho ho' (from Act III scene iv) in which he comes cross-gartered to Olivia believing that she loves him? Put together these aspects of Sir Toby and Malvolio and you come close to

Falstaff. What about Ollie as Falstaff, and Stan as Silence or Shallow, in the recruiting scene of Henry IV part ii, or Ollie in the Gadshill robbery of the first part, and in the tavern afterwards? Though there would have been problems in casting him for an actual production, Ollie's affinity with Falstaff is quite profound. They are childish father-figures, 'lovable rogues', at times demonstrably selfish and calculating, but thereby more fully human, and no less able to stand as embodiments of friendship, laughter, even love. The play between public respectability and subversion is similar in the two characters, and the two contexts. At the end of *A Chump at Oxford*, what Stan rejects explicitly is the insistence that (as we saw them doing at the start of the film) they swept the streets together, but by implication he is rejecting everything that 'Laurel and Hardy' stands for. He has become the (aristocratic) voice of responsibility shutting off the memory of the irresponsible times they had together, 'Stan, don't you know me?'/'Who is this coarse person with the foreign accent?'. Is this so far away from 'My king, my Jove, I speak to thee, my heart'/'I know thee not, old man . . .'? But Stan, finally, will meet Ollie's embrace.

To suggest that Laurel and Hardy have become objects of merely 'camp' affection, of a cult that will easily pass—next year perhaps Abbott and Costello, or Wheeler and Woolsey—is imperceptive. Their popular impact, irrespective of critical scorn or, more frequently, condescension, has been deep, lasting and justified. *A Chump at Oxford*, though not their best film, is their last at full pressure, and a worthy retrospect of their career and themes; it is their 'testament'; one loves it for its frailty as for its strength. Let us forget the decline of their later years, and leave them at this high point.

REPRISE

Still: Stan and Ollie as Two Tars *have picked up a couple of girls and taken them for a car ride. Hurrying to get back to their ship in time, they get stuck in a traffic jam. Driving the car behind is Edgar Kennedy.*

BACON GRABBERS

Stan and Ollie are deputies charged with serving a writ on Edgar Kennedy and attaching his radio. In order to place the document in his unwilling hand after he has locked them out, they borrow a ladder from a nearby building site and Stan climbs towards an open upstairs window. As the ladder is too short, Ollie has to lift it, and it lodges in the top of his trousers. The strain is too much for his braces. The deterrents escalate from mop to shot-gun, which misses Stan and hits a fire hydrant.

TOWED IN A HOLE

Stan has proved such a liability during the renovation of the boat that Ollie locks him in the cabin. While Ollie starts painting the mast, Stan tries to amuse himself and gets his head caught between the base of the mast and a bulkhead. He sets to work to free himself.

INDEX

The *last* number in each entry refers to the Filmography section.

FILMOGRAPHY

For the shorts, only the director credit is given.
Abbreviations are:
C.W. for *The Crazy World of Laurel & Hardy*
F.P. for *Further Perils of Laurel & Hardy*
L.T. for *Laurel & Hardy's Laughing 20s*

The only films listed, apart from three late ones made by Hardy, are those in which they appear together. Anything like a full analysis of their earlier careers is impossible, but McCabe, Coursodon and Borde & Perrin (see Bibliography) all list a fair number of 1913–26 titles. What proportion of their enormous output these make up, one can't tell.

These films were made by Hal Roach for his Comedy All Stars series, and distributed through Pathe:
1927: DUCK SOUP
SLIPPING WIVES. Directed by Fred Guiol.
LOVE EM AND WEEP. Directed by Fred Guiol.
WHY GIRLS LOVE SAILORS. Directed by Fred Guiol.
WITH LOVE AND HISSES. Directed by Fred Guiol.
SAILORS BEWARE. Directed by Fred Guiol.
DO DETECTIVES THINK? Directed by Fred Guiol. (Extracts in F.P.)
FLYING ELEPHANTS. Directed by Frank Butler. (Extracts in F.P.)

The next two films of the series were distributed through MGM, as were the rest of Roach's films up to 1939.
1927: SUGAR DADDIES. Directed by Fred Guiol. (Extracts in F.P.)
CALL OF THE CUCKOO. Directed by Clyde Bruckman.

The exact order and dating of films continues to be uncertain, right up to 1930. Films were not always released in the order they were made. But from now on they are all official Laurel & Hardy comedies.

My own rating of the shorts (those that I have seen in full, or nearly so) is indicated by the now conventional star method established by *Cahiers du Cinéma*. It translates roughly thus:
**** Great
*** Essential
** Worth Seeing
* Marginal
● Dud
When I have referred to a film at length in the text, the chapter number is given here.

1927: PUTTING PANTS ON PHILIP★★★
Directed by Clyde Bruckman
Hardy a respectable American citizen, Laurel his Scottish nephew. See Chapter 3.
Extracts in L.T.

1927: THE SECOND HUNDRED YEARS★★
Directed by Fred Guiol
Convicts. They escape from prison, change uniforms with some visiting French dignitaries, and dine formally at the Governor's before being identified.
Some dinner-table business is repeated in *From Soup to Nuts*. Stan with head shaved looks remarkably like Alec Guinness (e.g. in *The Prisoner*).
Extracts in F.P.
With James Finlayson (the Governor), Tiny Sanford (warder).

1927: HATS OFF
Directed by Hal Yates
Apparently a sketch for *The Music Box*, with Laurel and Hardy delivering a vacuum cleaner.

1927: THE BATTLE OF THE CENTURY
Directed by Clyde Bruckman
Stan starts as a boxer, Ollie as his manager. The final section is the pie-fight.
Extracts in L.T. and in *The Golden Age of Comedy*.
With Charley Hall (pieman), Anita Garvin (girl at end).

1928: LEAVE 'EM LAUGHING★★★
Directed by Clyde Bruckman
(1) in lodgings (2) at the dentist's (3) traffic chaos. See Chapter 5.
Extracts in L.T. and F.P.
With Charley Hall (landlord), Edgar Kennedy (policeman).

130

1928: THE FINISHING TOUCH**
Directed by Clyde Bruckman
Building a house. See Chapter 5. Extracts in L.T.
With Edgar Kennedy (policeman), Dorothy Coburn
(nurse).

1928: FROM SOUP TO NUTS***
Directed by Edgar Kennedy
Waiters at a society dinner-party. See Chapter 4.
The situation and some of the details are repeated in
A Chump at Oxford.
Extracts in L.T.
With Tiny Sanford (host), Anita Garvin (hostess),
Dorothy Coburn (guest).

1928: YOU'RE DARN TOOTIN' (*The Music
Blasters*)*******
Directed by Edgar Kennedy
Musicians. (1) concert (2) at lodgings (3) street chaos.
See Chapter 5.
Extracts in L.T. and F.P.

1928: THEIR PURPLE MOMENT***
Directed by James Parrott
The first film in which they are married. They desert
the wives and go to a nightclub, where they pick up two
girls. In the middle of a large dinner, they discover
they have no money with them. Soon, their wives
appear.
With Anita Garvin and Kay Deslys (the girls).

1928: SHOULD MARRIED MEN GO HOME?
Directed by James Parrott
Ollie is married. Stan calls on him and takes him to the
golf course. Clubs, turf and mud are soon flying.
The scene in which the Hardys, seeing Stan at the door,
pretend they are not at home is recreated in *Come Clean.*
Extracts in F.P.
With Kay Deslys (Mrs Hardy), Edgar Kennedy (golfer).

1928: EARLY TO BED****
Directed by Emmett Flynn
Ollie inherits a fortune; Stan becomes his servant. No
supporting cast. See Chapter 10.
Included nearly complete in F.P.

1928: TWO TARS****
Directed by James Parrott
Sailors on leave. They pick up two girls and go for a
country drive. Returning, they find themselves at the
head of a massive traffic jam. Irritation with their
neighbours swells into violence and spreads right down
the line of cars, creating one of the most exhilarating of
all their destruction scenes.

Extract in *The Golden Age of Comedy.*
With Charley Hall (shopkeeper), Edgar Kennedy and
Harry Bernard (drivers).

1928: HABEAS CORPUS
Directed by James Parrott
Hired as bodysnatchers, they climb into a graveyard at
dead of night.
Extracts in F.P.

1928: WE FAW DOWN (*We Slip Up*)
Directed by Leo McCarey
Both are married. An accident brings them to the
house of two other women; they are being looked after
when a boyfriend appears. They escape, only to meet
their own wives outside the window. The final image
is repeated at the end of *Blockheads:* a jealous wife's
rifle shot brings men leaping out of every window in the
block.
Extracts in C.W. and in *The Golden Age of Comedy.*
With Kay Deslys (the one with the boyfriend).

1929: LIBERTY****
Directed by Leo McCarey
Escaped convicts. See Chapter 4.
Included nearly complete in L.T.
With James Finlayson (shopkeeper).

1929: WRONG AGAIN****
Directed by Leo McCarey
Stable-boys; they deliver the horse 'Blue Boy' to a
millionaire's house. See Chapter 6.
Extracts in L.T.
With Harry Bernard (policeman).

1929: THAT'S MY WIFE***
Directed by Lloyd French
Mrs Hardy walks out on Ollie, provoked by the
behaviour of their lodger, Stan. Ollie's uncle arrives,
ready to leave him his money now that he's happily
married. Ollie makes Stan dress up as his wife, whom
the uncle hasn't met. They go to a nightclub for
dinner. Stan has costume difficulties; a drunk pursues
'her'; food is thrown. In the final shot Ollie, having
lost his legacy, stands unresisting as a bowl of soup is
tipped over his head by the drunk—a magnificent
stoicism that looks ahead to the end of *Helpmates.*
Nearly complete in F.P.
With Charley Hall and Harry Bernard (waiters).

1929: BIG BUSINESS****
Directed by James Horne

Christmas-tree salesmen. A masterpiece. See intro-ductory chapter.
Extracts in *When Comedy was King*.
With James Finlayson (householder), Tiny Sanford (policeman).

1929: DOUBLE WHOOPEE★★
Directed by Lewis Foster
Temporary hotel staff: they arrive, cause chaos, and leave.
A Prussian prince, modelled on Stroheim, falls repeatedly down a lift-shaft. Stan and Ollie sign the hotel register elaborately. They also (possibly for the first time) poke each other in the eye.
With Charley Hall (taxi-driver), Tiny Sanford (porter), Jean Harlow (girl with long dress).

1929: BERTH MARKS
Directed by Lewis Foster
Musicians. Travelling by train, they try to get to sleep in a narrow upper berth.

1929: BACON GRABBERS★★★
Directed by Lewis Foster
Sheriff's agents. They deliver a summons for non-payment of instalments on a radio.
Some brilliant acrobatic business as they try to get into the house.
Brief extracts in C.W.
With Edgar Kennedy (householder), Jean Harlow (his wife), Charley Hall (driver).

1929: ANGORA LOVE★★★
Directed by Lewis Foster
Followed back to their lodgings by a goat, they struggle to conceal it from their landlord. See Chapters 9 and 10.
The same situation is used in *Laughing Gravy* and *The Chimp*, with a dog and a monkey respectively.
Nearly complete in F.P.
With Edgar Kennedy (landlord), Charley Hall (fellow-lodger).

1929: UNACCUSTOMED AS WE ARE
Directed by Lewis Foster
This film, no longer available in England, is said to have been their first 100 per cent. talkie: hence the title. Some of the 1929 films listed above were apparently made in both sound and silent versions, but only the silent ones now circulate, whereas both *Men of War* and *The Perfect Day*—often, in fact, placed earlier in the year's list—have dialogue as an integral part.
With Edgar Kennedy (policeman).

1929: MEN OF WAR★★★★
Directed by Lewis Foster
Sailors. (1) They pick up two girls, (2) at the soda-fountain—see Chapter 9, (3) boating; sinking.
One of the shorts which has everything.
With James Finlayson (storekeeper), Harry Bernard (policeman), Charley Hall (man in boat).

1929: THE PERFECT DAY★★★★
Directed by James Parrott
Both are married. The families are setting out together for a picnic. When the car finally starts, it travels 100 yards before sinking into a mudhole. See Chapter 7.
With Edgar Kennedy (uncle), Kay Deslys (Mrs Hardy), Isabella Keith (Mrs Laurel), Daphne Pollard and Harry Bernard (neighbours).

1929: THEY GO BOOM
Directed by James Parrott
Ollie is ill in their lodgings.
With Charley Hall (landlord).

1929: THE HOOSEGOW★★★★
Directed by James Parrott
Convicts. See Chapter 8.
With James Finlayson (the Governor), Tiny Sanford (warder), Leo Willis (helpful convict), Charley Hall (sentry).

1930: NIGHT OWLS★★★
Directed by James Parrott
Vagrants. A policeman blackmails them into burgling his chief's house, so that he can arrest them and take the credit. They do so, waking the chief. The policeman mistimes his entrance and is taken for the burglar while they escape.
This is an incredibly inventive film. It consists almost entirely of their attempts to get into the house—a little ballet with walls, windows and doors.
With Edgar Kennedy (policeman), Anders Randolf (the chief), James Finlayson (Meadows, the butler).

1930: BLOTTO★★★
Directed by James Parrott
Stan is married, but not Ollie—a unique set-up. Ollie tempts him to come out to a nightclub; Stan undertakes to deceive his wife; but she, like Mrs Snagsby, sees it all. She replaces the bottle of liquor he is taking, saved from before Prohibition, with a concoction of cold tea, mustard, etc., and follows them to the club, buying a rifle en route. By now they are thoroughly drunk on her 'liquor', laughing helplessly. She chases them out, fires a shot at their getaway taxi and disintegrates it. (This final shot is in C.W.)

Another very rich film, not only in the drinking scene but in their subterfuges at the start: Ollie on the telephone, Stan sending himself a telegram but not being quite logical enough to carry through the deception consistently.

With Anita Garvin (Mrs Laurel), Tiny Sanford (waiter).

1930: BE BIG*
Directed by James Parrott

Both are married. Ollie feigns illness so that they can avoid a trip with the wives to Atlantic City and go to the club instead. After the wives have gone, Ollie gets one of Stan's boots on his foot and can't pull it off. This tugging takes up most of the film. The wives miss their train and arrive back to surprise them.

The main interest of this rather tame film is as a rehearsal for a section of *Sons of the Desert*.

With Mae Busch (Mrs Hardy), Anita Garvin (Mrs Laurel).

1930: BRATS**
Directed by James Parrott

The first of their double-role films: they play their own sons, disporting themselves within giant-sized replicas of the basic sets. Parents put children lovingly to bed but the children have left the bath running and the film ends with a flood.

Nothing much has 'happened' until this. By simply showing parents and children behaving alike, the film is making explicit the point about Stan and Ollie's essential childishness. In fact, the most childish acts are those of the parents, especially the way they play draughts and billiards. The technical contrivance is neat.

1930: THE LAUREL AND HARDY MURDER CASE ●
Directed by James Parrott

Vagrants. They read of an inheritance for which Stan may qualify and go together to a desolate house for the reading of the will. Strange things happen, but it was all a dream.

My candidate for the worst of their short films—perhaps in reaction against its popularity in terms of bookings, which is surely the result of a seductive title and nothing else.

1930: BELOW ZERO***
Directed by James Parrott

Musicians. Playing in the street, they do not meet with much luck, but they then find a bulging wallet. When a policeman protects them from a tough, they invite him out to a meal in gratitude. Having eaten, and persuaded him to let them pay, they notice that the wallet bears his photograph: they can't pay, and so are given the full treatment by the proprietor's hired toughs.

A very pure film, especially the first part. While the snow keeps falling, they play 'The Good Old Summertime' to an empty street. When they move on, we see Stan had been standing in front of a Deaf and Dumb Institute. Stan plays the harmonium, Ollie the double-bass: both instruments get smashed by an irate woman but they do little to resist. Nor, when they find the policeman's photo at the end, do they think to hide it. It is a film of passive, foredoomed suffering.

With Leo Willis (ruffian). In the street: Kay Deslys at the window, Vivien Oakland at the door, Charley Hall as the sweeper.

1930: HOG WILD (*Aerial Antics*)***
Directed by James Parrott

Ollie is married. His wife nags at him to put up a wireless aerial so that she can 'get Japan'. When Stan arrives on a visit, he volunteers to help. They make several ascents to the roof and Ollie has several falls. Finally he climbs up on a ladder rested on Stan's car. Stan starts the car accidentally and Ollie, on top of the ladder, is transported through the streets.

Basil Wright, a loyal and intelligent supporter of theirs during the thirties, has a comment on the central action which is worth recording, since the climax he describes has been cut from the version now available: 'In this film, the attempt to fix a wireless aerial on the roof of Hardy's house precipitated Hardy off the roof into the goldfish pond at least five times. Each time, a different gag-variation appeared, until the comedy passed into the realms of cutting, and the final fall was but a flight of birds and the sound of a mighty splash. Even Eisenstein would have been proud to do it.'

Other notable scenes are the start and end. Ollie searches furiously for his hat, which is on his head: Mrs Hardy's contempt is boundless. At the end, after he falls from the ladder, she joins them in the car for the ride back. The car gets crushed between two tramcars; but it still goes.

1930: ANOTHER FINE MESS***
Directed by James Parrott

Vagrants. They take refuge in a large house and impersonate the owner, showing round prospective tenants. The owner returns and they have to flee.

Stan has to dress up first as the butler and then as the maid, Agnes. As Agnes, he has an astonishing all-girls-together scene with Mrs Plumtree, talking intimately with her on the sofa. Ollie too has scope for unusual virtuosity. The plot framework is neatly done and it is a film which deserves to be better known.

In fact, Ollie's catch-phrase is invariably ' Well here's another *nice* mess you've gotten me into '.

With James Finlayson (the owner, Col. Buckshot) Thelma Todd (Mrs Plumtree), Harry Bernard (policeman).

1931: CHICKENS COME HOME ●
Directed by James Horne

Businessmen. Ollie is a candidate for mayor, Stan his assistant. Both are married. Ollie is embarrassed by the re-appearance of a woman from his past.

A remake of *Love 'em and Weep* (1927).

With Mae Busch (the vamp), James Finlayson (the Hardy butler).

1931: LAUGHING GRAVY ★★★★
Directed by James Horne

They are concealing a dog in their lodgings. On a freezing night, they have to fetch it in first from the garden, then from the roof. Ollie falls into a waterbutt and down the chimney. The enraged landlord finally expels them, but a policeman enters with news of quarantine: no-one may leave the house for two months. The landlord (offscreen) shoots himself.

Borde and Perrin give a mysteriously different version of the ending As they leave their lodgings, a telegram arrives: Stan's uncle has left him a fortune on condition that he abandons Hardy, who is responsible, we gather, for the level he has sunk to. This gives us one of the very rare scenes of sentiment in the whole of Laurel and Hardy. Finally, sentiment is dissolved in laughter when Stan refuses to abandon Ollie—not for the sake of their old friendship, but so that he won't lose the dog.' It's not that they have confused the film with any other of the sound shorts: *The Chimp*, a partial remake, does not end like this.

Can two versions of the ending have been made ?

In any case it is a consistently brilliant film.

With Charley Hall (landlord), Harry Bernard (policeman).

1931: OUR WIFE ★★★
Directed by James Horne

Ollie is getting married, Stan is his best man. The bride's father, seeing a photo of Ollie (the same one that is used eight years later in *Flying Deuces*), forbids the match: they therefore elope. A cross-eyed magistrate succeeds in marrying Stan to Ollie.

This is a fairly strict three-episode film. Preparations for marriage; elopement; at the magistrate's. The second section has an agonising scene as all three of them—and the bride is even larger than Ollie—pack

into the tiny car which Stan has hired for the occasion. The scene is a model of timing, getting the maximum number of laughs from the given situation: it's hard to see what Borde and Perrin mean when they call Horne, in this film and elsewhere, an inept director.

With James Finlayson (the bride's father), Ben Turpin (magistrate).

1931: COME CLEAN ★★
Directed by James Horne

Both are married. The men go out for ice-cream, and on their way back rescue a woman from drowning. She is far from grateful, and insists that they take her back to their apartment. They fail to shake her off, and so have to hide her from the wives.

Though the vamp figure is rather tedious, the domestic satire is sharp. And Stan especially has some inspired moments: bathing fully clothed, and revealing other depths of illogic. The film ends with a rare ' impossible ' gag: Ollie gets rid of Stan by letting out the bath water, and tells his wife that Stan has ' gone to the beach '.

With Mae Busch (the vamp), Charley Hall (ice-cream man), Gertrude Astor (Mrs Hardy).

1931: ONE GOOD TURN ★★
Directed by James Horne

Vagrants, calling themselves ' victims of the Depression '. Stan destroys their camping gear. Begging, they are taken in by a kind old woman. When they overhear the rehearsal of a play in which she takes the part of a hounded old widow, they resolve to help her save her home: they will sell their old car for $100 and surprise her with a gift. ' One Good Turn Deserves Another.' They don't get the money, and the car disintegrates under the weight of Stan and Ollie as they fight. Ollie thinks Stan has stolen the woman's purse and tells her. She puts them right about the play.

Clearly, this is one of the plots which gets unnecessarily in the way. Most of the second half is at low pressure, but there is some good detail in the first half, notably the camp scene. Stan, later, has a near-magical woodchopping game.

With Mary Carr (the woman), James Finlayson (the other actor), Billy Gilbert (drunk).

1931: BEAU CHUMPS (*Beau Hunks*) ★★★
Directed by James Horne

Legionnaires. Ollie joins up to forget the girl who has jilted him; Stan goes with him. After various failures to adapt to Army discipline, they defeat a Riffian attack by sprinkling tin-tacks under their (bare) feet as they enter the fort.

This is something of an experiment, being a pastiche of *Beau Geste*—Stan had made innumerable brief parodies in the twenties, *Rupert of Coleslaw* after *Rupert of Hentzau*, *Mud and Sand* after *Blood and Sand*, etc., and there are moments of pastiche in their other films together (*Double Whoopee*), but this is the only one on such a scale. It is also longer than normal, a step towards the feature-length films which begin in the same year. See Chapter 9. Extracts in C.W.

With Charles Middleton (the commandant—a part he repeats in *Flying Deuces*).

1931: HELPMATES****
Directed by James Parrott
Ollie is married; Mrs Hardy is away. On the morning she is due back, he asks Stan to come round and help clear up after a drunken party. Their efforts are repeatedly cancelled out by some fresh disaster. Eventually, with all his clothes destroyed, Ollie has to put on naval fancy dress to go and meet his wife. He returns with a black eye to find a shell, open to the elements, where once stood his house. (We saw Stan preparing to light the fire with liberally-poured petrol.) Ollie sits down in the ruins while Stan says goodbye. A storm begins.

An irreducible masterpiece. Brief extracts in C.W.

Three other characters appear in one shot each: postman, gardener, Mrs Hardy.

1932: ANY OLD PORT***
Directed by James Horne
Sailors on leave. The last of the distinct three-part films: (1) a quarrel with their landlord, (2) a restaurant scene: they are signed up for a boxing match, Ollie to manage, Stan to fight, (3) the fight. The opponent is the landlord. Stan wins.

The last section, in the boxing-ring, has the most skilful ' milking ' of a situation for gags in the whole of Laurel and Hardy. Extracts in C.W.

With Walter Long (landlord), Jacqueline Wells (his fiancee), Harry Bernard (impresario).

1932: THE MUSIC BOX****
Directed by James Parrott
The Laurel and Hardy Transfer Company, Foundered 1931. ' Tall Oaks from Little Acorns Grow '

They have to deliver an electric piano (bought by a woman as a surprise birthday present for her husband) to a house at the top of a long flight of steps. They unload it and carry it up. Twice it slides down again from half-way; once it slides down from the top. Having hauled it up again, they are shown a side-road that leads to the front door; they take the piano down the steps and bring it up by the road.

No-one is at home, but they take it inside (at the second attempt), set it up (after some damage to the furniture), and plug it in. They are dancing to its ' Medley of Patriotic Tunes ' when the owner, with whom they've already had an altercation on the steps, returns. He smashes the piano. His wife returns and tearfully explains about the surprise. He apologises and signs for delivery of the piano; but the pen lent him by Stan spurts ink in his face. They flee.

This won them their only Oscar (1932) and has always been their most celebrated film. Even those whose memory of Laurel and Hardy has grown dim with the years still remember *The Music Box*. It is the central symbol of the steps which gives it this power, the power of myth: it is ' the myth of Sisyphus in comic terms ' (Raymond Durgnat). Though the second half of the film is no anti-climax, it is the steps that are remembered.

Anthony Mann said of a conscious principle in his Westerns: ' The audience likes a man to say at the start "I am going to do this", and do it—because 90 per cent. of people in real life never accomplish what they hoped to do. In a film, if a character achieves the aim he set himself, the audience gets the feeling that it could have done the same, and feels closely identified with the character.'

Many Laurel and Hardy films are a comic inversion of this: they have a set thing to do and they fail. Given this principle, one might have expected other strong unifying symbols in their films, like these steps. But their normal manner is to work through a succession of details, charting the *process* of aspiration being thwarted and renewed—the focus of this aspiration, such as the house in *The Finishing Touch* or *Helpmates*, needs only to be felt in the background. In *The Music Box* the steps are there, and can't help having a persistent foreground emphasis; and they are ' used ' superbly.

The movement of the first half is delicately re-enacted in the second. At first they imagine the front door will be locked, so they winch the piano up to a first-floor balcony. They try to take it down the stairs but it falls out again; so they take it in the front door, which was open all along. And this is echoed once more in Ollie's movements: he goes upstairs to join Stan, Stan hears footsteps and calls out of the window, Ollie goes down again to answer and is told there is someone coming up the stairs. . . . This pattern of ' useless journeys ' gives the film a satisfying formal unity and is also a perfect enactment of Stan and Ollie's logic. Another formal excellence is in the editing, revealing a precise sense of when to cut a scene and move, with a slight ellipse, to the next. The economy of construction means that an enormous amount happens within the film's 25-minute length: it seems to have in it every-

thing that there is of Laurel and Hardy, including the greatest of all dance scenes. There is no reason to begrudge *The Music Box* its popularity.
Extracts in C.W. (sometimes out of sequence).
Charley Hall (postman), Billy Gilbert (householder).

1932: THE CHIMP ●
Directed by James Parrott
They work in a circus. When it breaks up the stock is shared out and they receive a chimp: they try to conceal it in their lodgings.
A half-hearted re-working of a familiar idea.
With James Finlayson (circus owner), Tiny Sanford (performer), Billy Gilbert (landlord).

1932: COUNTY HOSPITAL★★★
Directed by James Parrott
Stan, bearing hard-boiled eggs and nuts, visits Ollie in the hospital where he's recovering from a broken leg. The chaos he creates causes Ollie to be expelled. Stan has injected himself with sedative by mistake, so he falls asleep while he drives Ollie home.
After the excellence of the hospital scenes, the last section, based on very crude back-projection, is disappointingly mechanical.
With Billy Gilbert (surgeon).

1932: SCRAM★★★★
Directed by Raymond McCarey
Vagrants. A judge orders them out of town. They stop to help a drunk and are offered a bed by him on a rainy night. He instals them, discovers it's the wrong house, and leaves. Having made themselves at home, they encounter the woman of the house, who faints: they revive her with ' water ', in fact gin left behind by the drunk. She now wants to dance. While they are all laughing hysterically together on the bed, her husband returns—it's the judge who sentenced them. One of the three or four best shorts of the thirties, with no weakness. The same device is used here as in *Any Old Port* and *The Music Box* to give tightness to the plot: a sinister figure from the start is met unexpectedly at the end (cf. also *Going Bye-Bye*, below). The film has, in fact, moved from one grim close-up of the judge (his vindictive sentencing) to an almost identical final one, his long stare of anguish. It is a form of justice.
Ollie dominates the film. His shock at the idea of dancing with a married woman is deep and genuine; yet at the next moment, collapsed with laughter, he could be an allegorical representation of Irresponsibility.
With Richard Cramer (judge), Vivien Oakland (his wife), Arthur Housman (drunk).

136

1932: THEIR FIRST MISTAKE★★★★
Directed by George Marshall
Hardy is married. They adopt a baby. See Chapter 9.
With Mae Busch (Mrs Hardy), Billy Gilbert (process server).

1933: TOWED IN A HOLE★★★
Directed by George Marshall
Fishmongers. They buy and renovate a boat so that they can catch their own fish and ' eliminate the middleman '. At the end the boat, its sail unwisely hoisted, smashes both itself and their car.
The pattern is like that of *Busy Bodies* later in the year: complacent arrival in car, a series of precisely organised ' mechanical ' gags, destruction of car.
The film is more sophisticated than most, with a very slow pace and a scene where they discuss their relationship.
Extracts in C.W.

1933: TWICE TWO★★★
Directed by James Parrott (his last film for them)
Stan is married to the former Miss Hardy, played by Ollie. Ollie is married to the former Miss Laurel, played by Stan. They all share a house and the husbands share an office. The film has them coming home for a big anniversary dinner party together. It ends with Mrs Hardy crowning Mrs Laurel with a creamy gateau.
There appears to be only one process shot; otherwise it's all done with extreme skill by cutting. The wives' voices are dubbed. The situation makes for a very rich multiplication of the familiar Laurel Hardy tensions. Ollie, accustomed to playing himself opposite a female Laurel, here takes brilliantly his one chance in their films together to play in drag, and is the most memorable of the ' four '.
With Charley Hall (delivery boy).

1933: ME AND MY PAL★
Directed by Charles Rogers
Ollie is marrying, Stan is best man. Besides sending a wreath to the church, he brings Ollie a present in advance: a jigsaw. He starts doing it, others are drawn in, and they never get to the wedding. It ends in a fight with the police, the nearest thing to a mass-chaos scene after *The Hoosegow*.
A weak film, with a promising idea inadequately worked out.
With James Finlayson (bride's father).

1933: THE MIDNIGHT PATROL★★
Directed by Lloyd French

Policemen. They are sent to investigate a suspected burglary. It was in fact the police chief finding a way into his own house; but they break in, knock him out, and take him to the station. When he comes round, he shoots them (offscreen). ' Send for the coroner.'
With Charley Hall (criminal in car).

1933: BUSY BODIES★★★
Directed by Lloyd French
Carpenters, working in a large factory. Mostly they cause trouble for each other, but they also clash with workmates. It ends with their car being sliced in half by a mechanical saw—a scene which is said to have gone wrong and nearly killed them on the set.
The film is full of superbly opportunistic business with tools and machinery.
Extracts in C.W.
With Charley Hall (workmate), Tiny Sanford (foreman).

1933: DIRTY WORK★★
Directed by Lloyd French
Chimney-sweeps. They arrive at the house of a mad scientist who has just invented a youth elixir. Most of the film is good, predictable comedy based on the chimney-sweep situation. At the end, left alone in the laboratory, they decide to investigate the elixir, and Stan accidentally knocks Ollie into a bath full of it. He emerges as a chimp.
Brief extracts in C.W.

1934: THE PRIVATE LIFE OF OLIVER VIII★★
Directed by Lloyd French
Barbers (Stan still, however, goes to a shop down the road to get a shave). Ollie answers an advertisement and prepares to marry a mysterious rich widow. But she has a grudge against men called Oliver and has disposed of seven already; she is about to cut Ollie's throat when he wakes up.
A strange but quite a compelling film. The long dinner table scene, in which they are forced to eat imaginary food off imaginary plates, anticipates the final scene of Blow Up. Stan, true to his mode of dogged literalism, eventually breaks the spell by telling his hostess ' You're nuts '.
With Mae Busch (the widow).

1934: GOING BYE BYE★★
Directed by Charles Rogers
Their evidence has a criminal condemned; he swears vengeance. They decide to leave town and drive East. They advertise for a travelling companion and have an answer from a woman who turns out to be the criminal's

girl friend; when she finds he has broken out of prison she asks if she can bring him along too. It ends with mutual recognition and, before the police can catch him, he has carried out his earlier threat of twisting their legs around their necks. So, like Dirty Work, it ends on a ' freak ' image.
This is one of the films with an obtrusively complex plot. Stan and Ollie are at their best in the early scenes, in their own house. Later, the criminal is hiding in a locked trunk; his girl then asks them to get him out, explaining that he had been packing it and fell in. Stan and Ollie look at each other and consider, then Stan says decisively ' It could happen '.
With Mae Busch (the girl), Walter Long (the criminal).

1934: THEM THAR HILLS★★★★
Directed by Charles Rogers
Ollie has gout and, on doctor's orders, goes to the mountains with Stan. They park their caravan beside a well where we have just seen bootleggers, surprised by a police raid, emptying their liquor. They fetch in ' water ' from it to drink with supper. A married couple, who resemble the couple in Wild Strawberries, have run out of petrol and knock to ask for help. While the husband takes a filled can back to their car, his wife stays for supper. He returns to find them all drunk. His anger sets off a classic scene of retaliatory violence which ends with the collapse of the caravan and the ' explosion ' of Ollie from the alcoholic well, where he has fled to cool his blazing trousers.
A very rich film, the place of alcohol in which obviously recalls Scram. Some especially skilful acting (long takes) in the caravan scenes.
With Mae Busch (wife), Charley Hall (husband), Billy Gilbert (doctor).

1934: THE LIVE GHOST★★
Directed by Charles Rogers
Sailors. After being hired to shanghai others, they are themselves shanghaied and serve on a reputedly haunted ship whose captain forbids them to mention the word ghost. The combination of a drunken mate and their own bungling leads them to ' see ' a ghost and tell the captain; he carries out his threat of twisting their heads back to front.
With Walter Long (captain), Arthur Housman (mate).

1935: TIT FOR TAT★★★
Directed by Charles Rogers
Shopkeepers. The film is a sequel to Them Thar Hills. Stan and Ollie set up as electricians and find that the grocer and his wife, next door, are the couple

they met before. Ollie's (typically generous) offer of friendship is rejected by Mr Hall, and they are soon engaged in destroying each other's stock, etc.

Such is their concentration on the job in hand that they ignore a little man who keeps passing them on his way into their shop, where he methodically steals the contents. Ollie says ' Come on, we've got more important things to think about ' At the end, he leaves in a removal van.

With Charley Hall (the Grocer), Mae Busch (his wife), Harry Bernard (policeman).

1935: THE FIXER UPPERS*
Directed by Charles Rogers
Christmas Card salesmen. A French artist catches Ollie in a compromising situation with his wife and challenges him to a duel. They try to evade it but fail.
With Charles Middleton (the artist), Mae Busch (his wife), Arthur Housman (drunk).

1935: THICKER THAN WATER**
Directed by James Horne
Ollie is married, Stan is the lodger. Mrs Hardy attacks them for their confusion over money, which has led to an irate visit from the man to whom they are paying instalments on the furniture. The two men have the idea of drawing out the Hardy savings of $300 from the bank and buying the furniture outright. On their way to pay they are tempted into an auction where they unwittingly buy, for $290, a grandfather clock—they then put it down in the road to take a rest, and see it run over. Arriving home, Ollie is beaten up by his wife.

In hospital, Stan comes to visit him and is made to give blood. Something goes wrong and blood has to be taken back from Ollie and pumped into Stan. ' The end, after this exchange, is horribly complex. Ollie is made up as Stan and speaks with Stan's voice (dubbed) explaining that he couldn't help it—i.e. Ollie-playing-Stan represents Stan-with-Ollie's-blood. But because the operation has made him look like Ollie, he is called Mr Hardy by the nurse. And vice-versa: Stan is made up as Ollie, with Ollie's voice, to represent a shrunken Ollie.

Apart from this bizarre ending to their career in short films, the best part is·their washing-up routine near the start. This is included in C.W.

The auction scene is remade in *Dancing Masters* (1943). With James Finlayson (shopkeeper), Daphne Pollard (Mrs Hardy), Charley Hall (cashier).

138

Features:

1931: PARDON US (*Jailbirds*) Hal Roach/MGM
Directed by James Parrott. Script by H. M. Walker. Photographed by Jack Stevens. With Wilfred Lucas (governor), James Finlayson (teacher), Charley Hall (dentist), Tiny Sanford (warder), Walter Long and Leo Willis (convicts).

1932: PACK UP YOUR TROUBLES Hal Roach/MGM
Directed by George Marshall and Raymond McCarey. Script by H. M. Walker. Photographed by Art Lloyd. With James Finlayson (General), George Marshall (cook), Jacqui Lyn (orphan), Richard Cramer (her guardian), Billy Gilbert (bride's father), Charles Middleton (welfare officer).

1933: FRA DIAVOLO (*The Devil's Brother*) Hal Roach/MGM
Directed by Hal Roach and Charles Rogers. Script by Jeannie MacPherson (from the opera by Frank Auber). Photographed by Art Lloyd and Hap Depew. With Dennis King (Fra Diavolo), James Finlayson (Lord Rocburg), Thelma Todd (Lady Pamela Rocburg), Henry Armetta (landlord), Wilfred Lucas (Alessandro), Tiny Sanford, Kay Deslys.

1933: SONS OF THE DESERT (*Sons of the Legion—Fraternally Yours—Convention City*) Hal Roach/MGM
Directed by William A. Seiter. Script by Frank Craven and Byron Morgan. Photographed by Kenneth Peach. With Mae Busch (Mrs Hardy), Dorothy Christie (Mrs Laurel), Charley Chase (Mr Chase).

1934: BABES IN TOYLAND (*Wooden Soldiers*) Hal Roach/MGM
Directed by Gus Meins and Charles Rogers. Script by Nick Grinde and Frank Butler (from the operetta by Victor Herbert with book and lyrics by Glen MacDonough). Photographed by Art Lloyd and Francis Corby. With Henry Brandon (Barnaby), Charlotte Henry (Bo-Peep).

1935: BONNIE SCOTLAND Hal Roach/MGM
Directed by James Horne. Script by Frank Butler and Jeff Moffitt. Photographed by Art Lloyd and Francis Corby. With James Finlayson (Sergeant), Daphne Pollard (Millie), Vernon Steel (Col. McGregor), Anne Grey (Lady Violet Ormsby), June Lang (Lorna MacLaurel).

1936: THE BOHEMIAN GIRL Hal Roach/MGM
Directed by James Horne and Charles Rogers. Script by Alfred Bunn (from the opera by Michael W. Balfe). Photographed by Art Lloyd and Francis Corby. With James Finlayson (Captain Finn), Jacqueline Wells (Princess Arline), William P. Carleton (Count Arnheim), Mae Busch (Mrs Hardy), Antonio Moreno (her lover). Extracts in C.W.

1936: OUR RELATIONS Hal Roach/MGM A Stan Laurel Production
Directed by Harry Lachman. Script by Richard Connell and Felix Adler; adapted by Charles Rogers and Jack Jevne from 'The Money Box' by W. W. Jacobs. Photographed by Rudolph Maté. With Daphne Pollard (Mrs Hardy), Betty Healy (Mrs Laurel) James Finlayson (fellow-sailor), Alan Hale (Grogan), Sidney Toler (Captain), Arthur Housman (drunk).

1937: WAY OUT WEST Hal Roach/MGM A Stan Laurel Production
Directed by James Horne. Script by Jack Jevne, Felix Adler, Charles Rogers, James Parrott. Photographed by Art Lloyd and Walter Lundin. With James Finlayson (Mickey Finn), Sharon Lynne (Lola Marcel), Rosina Lawrence (Mary Roberts), Stanley Fields (Sheriff), Vivien Oakland (his wife), Harry Bernard (man with steak).
Extracts in C.W.

1938: SWISS MISS Hal Roach/MGM
Directed by John G. Blystone. Script by James Parrott, Charles Melson and Felix Adler, from a story by Jean Negulesco and Charles Rogers. Photographed by Norbert Brodine and Art Lloyd. With Della Lind (Anna), Walter Woolf King (Victor), Eric Bloor (Edward), Charles Gamore (gorilla).
Extracts in C.W.

1938: BLOCKHEADS Hal Roach/MGM
Directed by John G. Blystone. Script by James Parrott, Harry Langdon, Felix Adler, Charles Rogers, Arnold Belgard. Photographed by Art Lloyd. With Billy Gilbert (Mr Gilbert), Patricia Ellis (Mrs Gilbert), Minna Gombell (Mrs Hardy), James Finlayson (Mr Finn).

1939: FLYING DEUCES Boris Morros/RKO Radio
Directed by Edward Sutherland. Script by Ralph Spence, Charles Rogers, Alfred Schiller, Harry Langdon. Photographed by Art Lloyd. With Jean Parker (Georgette), Reginald Gardiner (her husband), James Finlayson (Sergeant), Charles Middleton (**Commandant**).

1940: A CHUMP AT OXFORD Hal Roach/United Artists
Directed by Alfred Goulding. Script by Charles Rogers, Felix Adler, Harry Langdon. Photographed by Art Lloyd. With Wilfred Lucas (Dean), Forrester Harvey (Meredith), James Finlayson and Anita Garvin (society couple), Charley Hall and Peter Cushing (students), Harry Bernard (policeman).

1940: SAPS AT SEA Hal Roach/United Artists
Directed by Gordon Douglas. Script by Charles Rogers, Harry Langdon, Gil Pratt, Felix Adler. Photographed by Art Lloyd. With Richard Cramer (convict), James Finlayson (doctor), Ben Turpin (plumber), Charley Hall (porter), Harry Bernard (policeman).

1941: GREAT GUNS Fox Directed by Monty Banks

1942: A HAUNTING WE WILL GO Fox Directed by Alfred Werker

1943: AIR RAID WARDENS MGM Directed by Edward Sedgwick

1943: JITTERBUGS Fox Directed by Malcolm St Clair

1943: DANCING MASTERS Fox Directed by Malcolm St Clair

1944: THE BIG NOISE Fox Directed by Malcolm St Clair

1944: NOTHING BUT TROUBLE MGM Directed by Sam Taylor

1945: THE BULLFIGHTERS Fox Directed by Malcolm St Clair

1951: ATOLL K (*Robinson Crusoeland—Utopia*) Fortezza/Sirius Directed by Leo Joannon

Other films together:
1917: LUCKY DOG
Directed by Jesse Robbins
A chance association.

1926: 45 MINUTES FROM HOLLYWOOD
They appear separately in this medley, which pre-dates the other films that they made for Roach.
Brief extract in L.T.

1929: HOLLYWOOD REVUE OF 1929 MGM (sound)
Directed by Charles Reisner
A short set-piece, on their own. Hardy as a conjuror, whose tricks Laurel ruins.

1930: ROGUE SONG MGM Technicolor
Directed by Lionel Barrymore
Some Laurel and Hardy scenes were cut in, as an afterthought, to provide comic relief in this vehicle for the opera star, Lawrence Tibbett. Unfortunately, no copy is available, so we can't see what they look like in colour (Stan had red hair).

1934: HOLLYWOOD PARTY OF 1934 MGM
Directed by Richard Boleslawski
Another musical comedy revue. Laurel and Hardy's section is. said to be included in *MGM's Big Parade of Laughs*, not released in England.

1937: PICK A STAR MGM
Directed by Edward Sedgwick
Starlets visit Hollywood and meet, among others, Laurel and Hardy.

Hardy on his own:
1939: ZENOBIA (*Elephants Never Forget*) Hal Roach/United Artists
Directed by Gordon Douglas
Hardy's contract with Roach ran for a few months longer than Laurel's. When Roach cast him here with Harry Langdon, he unwittingly started rumours of a new Langdon-and-Hardy partnership.

1949: THE FIGHTING KENTUCKIAN Republic
Directed by George Waggner
With John Wayne.

1950: RIDING HIGH Paramount
Directed by Frank Capra
With Bing Crosby and Charles Bickford.

Compilation films:

1957: THE GOLDEN AGE OF COMEDY Robert Youngson/DCA
Has extracts from *The Second Hundred Years, The Battle of the Century, We Faw Down* and *Two Tars*.

1959: WHEN COMEDY WAS KING Robert Youngson/Fox
Ends with a shortened version of *Big Business*.

1961: DAYS OF THRILLS AND LAUGHTER Robert Youngson/Fox
Includes some material from their respective early careers.

1962: THIRTY YEARS OF FUN Robert Youngson/Fox
Has their first screen meeting, from *Lucky Dog* (1917).

1964: MGM's BIG PARADE OF LAUGHS Robert Youngson/MGM
See above (*Hollywood Party of 1934*).

1965: LAUREL AND HARDY'S LAUGHING 20s Robert Youngson/MGM
Long extracts from *Putting Pants on Philip, The Finishing Touch, From Soup to Nuts, Liberty* and *Wrong Again*. Shorter ones from *The Battle of the Century, Leave 'em Laughing* and *You're Darn Tootin'*. Also some 'flashes' of much earlier material.

1966: THE CRAZY WORLD OF LAUREL AND HARDY A Jay Ward Production
A large number of sound shorts are covered, but the only ones of which we get more than brief flashes are *Beau Chumps, Any Old Port, The Music Box, Towed in a Hole* and *Busy Bodies*. Also pieces from three of the feature films: *The Bohemian Girl, Way out West* and *Swiss Miss*.

1967: FURTHER PERILS OF LAUREL AND HARDY Robert Youngson/Fox
More material from their early careers; also extracts from *Do Detectives Think?, Flying Elephants, Sugar Daddies, The Second Hundred Years, Leave 'em Laughing, You're Darn Tootin', Should Married Men Go Home?, Early to Bed, Habeas Corpus, That's My Wife!*, and *Angora Love*.

SOURCES

Compiled by Robert Wade Chatterton

Key to symbols:
R = Rental sources
S = Sale sources
8 = 8mm, silent
8 + = 8mm, magnetic sound
16 = 16mm, silent
16 + = 16mm, optical sound
T = Prerecorded taped score for sale
NA = Not available at present
No gauge symbol = film not yet available

Key to source firms: (main offices only)
A Audio Film Center, 34 MacQueston Parkway S., Mt. Vernon, New York 10550
B Blackhawk Films, Eastin-Phelan Corp., Davenport, Iowa 52808
BF Budget Films, 4950 Santa Monica Blvd., Los Angeles, Cal. 90029
BR Brandon Films, 221 West 57th St., New York, N.Y. 10019
C Cinema Arts Society, P.O. Box 85363, Hollywood, Cal. 90072
CO Cooper's Rental Service, Northedge Shopping Center, Eaton, Ohio 45320
CR Creative Film Society, 14558 Valerio St., Van Nuys, Cal. 91405
E Entertainment Films Company, 350 Seventh Ave., New York, N.Y. 10019
EX Essex Film Club, 263 Harrison St., Nutley, N.J. 07110
F Film Classic Exchange, 1926 S. Vermont Ave., Los Angeles, Cal. 90007
FI Films, Inc., 425 N. Michigan Ave., Chicago, Ill. 60611
I Institutional Cinema Service, 29 E. 10th St., New York, N.Y. 10003
J Jack Hardy, P.O. Box 813, Clarksville, Va. 23927
S Select Film Library, 138 East 44th St., New York, N.Y. 10017
SW Swank Motion Pictures, 201 S. Jefferson Ave., St. Louis, Mo. 63205
W Westcoast Films, 255 Minna St., San Francisco, Cal. 94103

Duck Soup NA
Slipping Wives NA
Love Em and Weep **R:** BF(16), F(16+) **S:** F(8,16+)
Why Girls Love Sailors NA
With Love and Hisses **R:** A, BF(16), F(16+) **S:** F(8,16+)
Sailors Beware **R:** F(16+) **S:** F(8,16+)
Do Detectives Think? **R:** BF, SW(16), F(16+) **S:** F(8,16+) **T:** J
Flying Elephants **R:** A(16) **S:** NA **T:** EX
Sugar Daddies **R:** F(16+), CO(8) **S:** B(8,16), F(8,16+)
Call of the Cuckoo **R:** CO(8) **S:** B(8,16)
Putting Pants on Philip **R:** A,CR,BF,SW(16), CO(8) **S:** B(8,16) **T:** EX
The Second Hundred Years **R:** A(16), CO(8) **S:** B(8,16)
Hats Off **R:** NA **S:** B
The Battle of the Century **R:** NA **S:** B
Leave 'em Laughing **R:** A,BF(16), CO(8) **S:** B(8,16) **T:** EX
The Finishing Touch **R:** A,BF(16), CO(8) **S:** B(8,16) **T:** EX

141

From Soup to Nuts **R:** BF,SW(16), CO(8) **S:** B(8,16)

You're Darn Tootin' **R:** A,CR,SW(16), CO(8) **S:** B(8,16)

Their Purple Moment **R:** CO(8) **S:** B(8,16)

Should Married Men Go Home ? **R:** NA **S:** B

Early to Bed **R:** BF(16), CO(8) **S:** B(8)

Two Tars **R:** A,BF,CR,SW(16), CO(8) **S:** B(8,16) **T:** EX

Habeas Corpus **R:** NA **S:** B

We Faw Down **R:** CO(8) **S:** B(8)

Liberty **R:** NA **S:** B

Wrong Again **R:** CO(8) **S:** B(8,16) **T:** EX

That's My Wife **R:** NA **S:** B

Big Business **R:** A,BF,CR(16), CO(8) **S:** B(8,16)

Double Whoopee **R:** A,CR(16), CO(8) **S:** B(8,16) **T:** EX

Berth Marks **R:** CO(8,8+) **S:** B(8,8+,16,16+)

Bacon Grabbers **R:** A,BF(16), CO(8) **S:** B(8,16)

Angora Love **R:** CO(8) **S:** B(8+,16+)

Unaccustomed As We Are **R:** CO(8,8+) **S:** B(8,8+,16+)

Men Of War **R:** A,SW,W(16+), CO(8+) **S:** B(8,8+,16+)

The Perfect Day **R:** A,BF,I,SW(16+), CO(8+) **S:** B(8+,16+)

They Go Boom **R:** NA **S:** B

The Hoosegow **R:** I(16+) **S:** B

Night Owls **R:** F,I,W(16+) **S:** B(16+), F(8,16+)

Blotto **R:** BF,I(16+), CO(8+) **S:** B(8+,16+)

Be Big **R:** BF,I,SW,W(16+), CO(8+) **S:** B(8+,16+)

Brats **R:** A,BF,I,SW,W(16+), CO(8+) **S:** B(8+,16+)

The Laurel and Hardy Murder Case **R:** BF,SW,W(16+), CO(8+) **S:** B 8,8+,16+)

Below Zero **R:** A,BF,SW,W(16+), CO(8+) **S:** B(8+,16+)

Hog Wild **R:** F,I,SW,W(16+), CO(8+) **S:** B(8+,16+), F(8,16)

Another Fine Mess **R:** BF,I,W(16+), CO(8+) **S:** B(8+,16+)

Chickens Come Home **R:** BF,I,W(16+), CO(8+) **S:** B(8+,16+)

Laughing Gravy **R:** A,BF,I(16+) **S:** B

Our Wife **R:** CR,I,SW,W(16+), CO(8+) **S:** B(8+,16+)

Come Clean **R:** CO(8+) **S:** B(8+,16+)

One Good Turn **R:** BF,I,SW,W(16+), CO(8+) **S:** B(8+,16+)

Beau Chumps **R:** A,BF,SW,W(16+), CO(8+) **S:** B(8+,16+)

Helpmates **R:** SW,W(16+), CO(8+) **S:** B(8+, 16+)

Any Old Port **R:** B,I,W(16+), CO(8+) **S:** B(8+,16+)

The Music Box **R:** A,BF,CR,I,W(16+), CO(8+) **S:** B(8,8+,16+)

The Chimp **R:** BF,I,W(16+), CO(8+) **S:** B(8+, 16+)

County Hospital **R:** BF,CR,I,W,(16+), CO(8+) **S:** B(8+,16+)

Scram **R:** BF,I,SW(16+) **S:** B(16+

Their First Mistake **R:** BF,F,I(16+), CO(8+) **S:** B(8+,16+), F(8,16+)

Towed in a Hole **R:** A,BF,SW,W(16+), CO(8+) **S:** B(8,8+,16+)

Twice Two **R:** BF,I,SW,W(16+), CO(8+) **S:** B(8+,16+)

Me And My Pal **R:** I,SW,W(16+), CO(8+) **S:** B(8+,16+)

The Midnight Patrol **R:** SW,W(16+), CO(8+) **S:** B(8+,16+)

Busy Bodies **R:** A,BF,I,SW,W(16+), CO(8+) **S:** B(8+,16+)

Dirty Work **R:** BF,I,SW,W(16+), CO(8+) **S:** B(8+,16+)

The Private Life Of Oliver VIII **R:** BF,I,SW,W (16+), **S:** B(16+)

Going Bye Bye **R:** W(16+) **S:** B(16+)

Them Thar Hills **R:** BF,I,W(16+), CO(8,8+) **S:** B(8,8+,16+)

The Live Ghost **R:** BF,SW,W(16+), CO(8+) **S:** B(8+,16+)

Tit For Tat **R:** BF,F,I,SW,W(16+), CO(8,8+) **S:** B(8,8+,16+), F(8,16+)

The Fixer Uppers **R:** BF,I,W(16+) **S:** B

Thicker Than Water **R:** BF,I,SW,W(16+) **S:** B(16+)

Pardon Us **R:** A,S(16+), CO(8+) **S:** B(8+,16+)

Pack Up Your Troubles **R:** A,BF,S(16+), CO(8+) **S:** B,E(8+,16+)

Fra Diavolo **NA**

Sons Of The Desert **R:** A,BF,S(16+) **S:** E(16+), B

Babes In Toyland **R:** A,I,WS,W(16+) **S:** NA
Bonnie Scotland **R:** BF(16+) **S:** NA
The Bohemian Girl **R:** R(16+), BF, CO(8+)
S: B(8+,16+)
Our Relations **R:** A,BF,W(16+) **S:** B(16+)
Way Out West **R:** A,S,SW,W(16+), CO(8+)
S: B(8+,16+)
Swiss Miss **R:** A,BR,S,W(16+), CO(8+) **S:**
E(8+,16+), B
Blockheads **R:** BF,S,SW,W(16+), CO(8+) **S:**
B(8+,16+)
Flying Deuces **R:** S,W(16+), BF **S:** NA
A Chump at Oxford **R:** BR,I,S,SW,W(16+),
CO(8+) **S:** B(8, 8+,16+)
Saps at Sea **R:** BF,BR,I,S,SW,W(16+), CO(8+)
S: B(8,8+,16+)
Great Guns **R:** FI(16+), **S:** NA
A Haunting We Will Go **R:** A,BF,W(16+) **S:** NA
Air Raid Wardens **R:** FI(16+) **S:** NA
Jitterbugs **R:** FI(16+) **S:** NA
Dancing Masters **R:** A(16+) **S:** NA
The Big Noise **R:** BF,W(16+) **S:** NA
Nothing But Trouble **R:** FI(16+) **S:** NA
The Bullfighters **R:** FI(16+) **S:** NA
Atoll K NA
Lucky Dog **R:** BF(16) **S:** BF(16)
45 Minutes From Hollywood NA
Hollywood Revue of 1929 MGM NA
Rogue Song MGM NA
Hollywood Party of 1934 MGM NA
Pick a Star MGM NA, but one sequence titled
A Day at the Studio rents from BF(16+)
Zenobia **R:** S(16+) **S:** NA
The Fighting Kentuckian NA
Riding High NA
The Golden Age of Comedy **R:** A,BF,SW(16+)
S: NA
When Comedy was King **R:** A,BF,SW(16+)
S: NA
Days of Thrills and Laughter **R:** FI,SW(16+)
S: NA
Thirty Years of Fun **R:** FI(16+) **S:** NA
MGM's Big Parade of Laughs **R:** FI(16+) **S:** NA
Laurel and Hardy's Laughing 20s NA
The Crazy World of Laurel and Hardy NA
Further Perils of Laurel and Hardy **R:** FI(16+)
S: NA

Bibliography

Books
BORDE, Raymond and PERRIN, Charles: *Laurel et Hardy*. Premier Plan, September 1965.
COURSODON, Jean-Pierre: *Laurel et Hardy*. Anthologie du Cinéma, October 1965.
EVERSON, William K: *The Films of Laurel and Hardy*. Citadel N.Y. 1967.
McCABE, John: *Mr Laurel and Mr Hardy*. Doubleday N.Y. 1961; new edition, Grosset and Dunlap N.Y. 1966.

Books with relevant chapters
AGEE, James: *Agee on Film*. Obolensky N.Y. 1958. Essay on ' Comedy's Greatest Era ' in volume 1.
COURSODON, Jean-Pierre: *Keaton & Co, Les Burlesques Americains du ' muet '*. Editions Seghers 1964. Chapter on ' Laurel and Hardy '.
GRIERSON, John: *Grierson on Documentary*. Collins 1946; new edition, Faber 1966. Essay on ' The Logic of Comedy '.

Magazine pieces
BARNES, Peter: ' Cuckoo ', article on Laurel and Hardy in *Films and Filming*, August 1960.
DANEY, Serge and NOAMES, Jean-Louis: Interview with Leo McCarey in *Cahiers du Cinéma*, February 1965.
DURGNAT, Raymond: ' Hoop-de-Doo for Mr L and Mr H ', article on film comedians in *Films and Filming*, November 1965.
MARS, François: ' Lorèléardi est mort ', article following Hardy's death, in *Cahiers du Cinéma*, October 1957.
ROBINSON, David: (1) ' The Lighter People ', article on Laurel and Hardy in *Sight and Sound*, Summer 1954. (2) Review of John McCabe's book in *Sight and Sound*, Winter 1961-2.
VERB, Boyd: Interview with Stan Laurel in *Films in Review*, March 1959.
WRIGHT, Basil: (1) ' Blest Pair of Sirens ', article on Laurel and Hardy in *World Film News*, June 1937. (2) Review of *Way out West* in *World Film News*, January 1938. (3) Review of *Blockheads* in *World Film News*, October 1938.